W9-CCF-253

Get Ready! for Social Studies
GEOGRAPHY

Books in the *Get Ready! for Social Studies* Series:

Essays, Book Reports, and Research Papers
Geography
Government and Citizenship
U.S. History
World History

Nancy White and Francine Weinberg, series editors, have been involved in educating elementary and secondary students for more than thirty years. They have had experience in the classroom as well as on dozens of books and electronic projects. They welcome this partnership with parents and other adults to promote knowledge, skills, and critical thinking.

Get Ready! for Social Studies
GEOGRAPHY

Nancy Furstinger
Rena B. Korb
Richard A. Miller

Series Editors
Nancy White
Francine Weinberg

McGraw-Hill
New York   Chicago   San Francisco
Lisbon   London   Madrid   Mexico City
Milan   New Delhi   San Juan   Seoul
Singapore   Sydney   Toronto

Library of Congress Cataloging-in-Publication Data applied for.

McGraw-Hill

*A Division of The **McGraw·Hill** Companies*

1 2 3 4 5 6 7 8 9 0   QPD/QPD   0 9 8 7 6 5 4 3 2

ISBN 0-07-137761-1

This book was set in Goudy Oldstyle by North Market Street Graphics.

Printed and bound by Quebecor/Dubuque.

Maps on pages 28–31 and 132–147 © – **MAPQUEST.** –

McGraw-Hill books are available at special quantity discounts to use as premiums and sales promotions, or for use in corporate training programs. For more information, please write to the Director of Special Sales, Professional Publishing, McGraw-Hill, Two Penn Plaza, New York, NY 10121-2298. Or contact your local bookstore.

 This book is printed on recycled, acid-free paper containing a minimum of 50% recycled, de-inked fiber.

Contents

Introduction

In recent years, the media have told us that many students need to know more about history, geography, and government and to improve their writing skills. While schools are attempting to raise standards, learning need not be limited to the classroom. Parents and other concerned adults can help students too. *Get Ready! for Social Studies* provides you with the information and resources you need to help students with homework, projects, and tests and to create a general excitement about learning.

You may choose to use this book in several different ways, depending on your child's strengths and preferences. You might read passages aloud, you might read it to yourself and then paraphrase it for your child, or you might ask your child to read the material along with you or on his or her own. To help you use this book successfully, brief boldface paragraphs, addressed to you, the adult, appear from time to time.

Here is a preview of the features you will find in each chapter.

Word Power

To help students expand their vocabulary, the "Word Power" feature in each chapter defines underlined words with which students may be unfamiliar. These are words that students may use in a variety of contexts in their writing and speaking. In addition, proper nouns and more technical terms appear in boldface type within the chapter, along with their definitions. For example, the word decade is defined as "period of ten years" on a "Word Power" list. The word **cartography** would appear in boldface type within the chapter and be defined there as "the science of mapmaking."

What Your Child Needs to Know

This section provides key facts and concepts in a conversational, informal style to make the content accessible and engaging for all readers.

Implications

This section goes beyond the facts and concepts. Here, we provide the answers to students' centuries-old questions, "Why does this matter?" and "Why is this important for me to know?"

Fact Checker

A puzzle, game, or other short-answer activity checks children's grasp of facts—people, places, things, dates, and other details.

The Big Questions

These questions encourage students to think reflectively and critically in order to form a broader understanding of the material.

Skills Practice

Activities provide the opportunity for children to learn and to apply reading, writing, and thinking skills basic to social studies and other subjects as well. These skills include learning from historical documents, map reading, identifying cause and effect, comparing and contrasting, and writing analytically and creatively.

Top of the Class

In this section, creative suggestions help students stand out in class. By taking some of these suggestions, students can show their teachers that they have been putting in the extra effort that means the difference between average and excellent performance.

The book you are now holding in your hand is a powerful tool. It will help you boost your child's performance in school, increase his or her self-confidence, and open the door to a successful future as a well-educated adult.

When you look at maps with your child, please remember that, because the world is constantly in flux, international borders and even names of countries change from time to time. New facts and theories about history surface as well.

Nancy White and Francine Weinberg

CHAPTER 1
Geography Matters

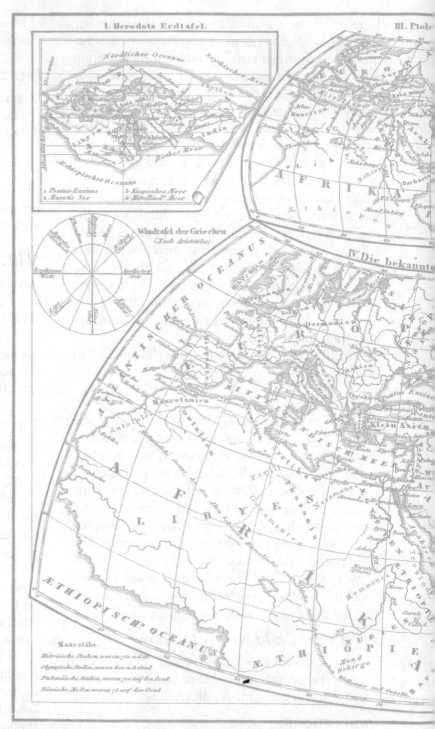

Ancient maps by Herodotus, Ptolemy, and others

Geographic facts are part of our world all the time, but we may not think much about them. Where and how we live, what we eat, how we think and talk, how we dress and move about, and other decisions depend on geography. Throughout history, geography has made its mark on us, and we have tried to conquer geography, as the following pages show.

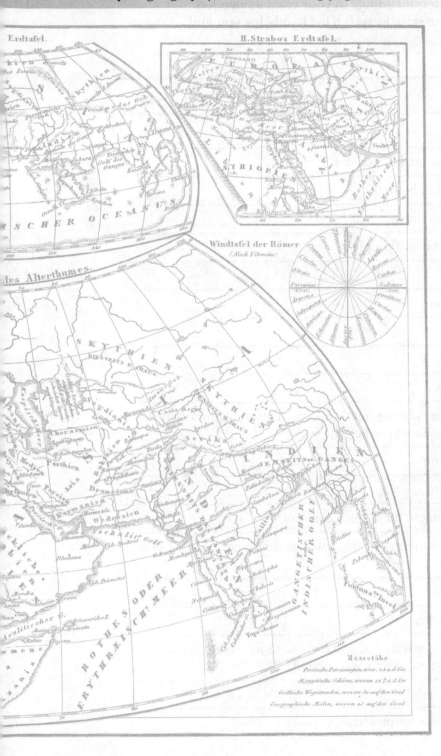

Word Power

The words on the following chart are underscored in the section called "What Your Child Needs to Know." Explain their meanings to your child as needed when they come up in reading or discussion. Keep the list handy for you and your child to use.

Word	*Definition*
accelerated	sped-up
arsenal	place where weapons are built or stored
boundaries	things marking a limit; borders
circumference	distance around something
cultural	related to the way of life of people
decade	period of ten years
emerging	arising; coming about
expeditions	long trips
exploited	treated unfairly
foundered	broke down; collapsed
hypothesized	came up with a theory about something, based on some information; made an educated guess or prediction
isolate	keep separate or alone
literate	able to read and write
motivation	reason or encouragement for doing something
navigational	related to using instruments or other information to go from one place to another
pollute	make dirty or impure
relevant	directly concerned with
resources	things that a country or state has and can use to its advantage (for example, the natural resources coal and oil)
systematic	organized; orderly
technological	related to using science for practical purposes
urban	related to cities

What Your Child Needs to Know

You may choose to use the following text in several different ways, depending on your child's strengths and preferences. You might read the passage aloud; you might read it to yourself and then paraphrase it for your child; or you might ask your child to read the material along with you or on his or her own.

WHAT IS GEOGRAPHY?

In simplest terms, *geography* is "earth writing"; that's what it means in Greek (*geo* meaning "earth," "ground," or "soil," and *graph* meaning "writing"). Looking back to the centuries just before the birth of Christ, we see that the ancient Greeks deserve to be called the first geographers because they made careful studies of the world around them. They estimated distances from one place to another and, hundreds of years before scientists would prove the fact, <u>hypothesized</u> that the planet Earth is round.

A more thorough definition of geography is "the study and explanation of Earth, its <u>resources</u>, and life, with particular emphasis on the description of the land, air, and water, and the distribution of plants, animals, and people." For example, when we read about people building trading towns along a river and then about how the townspeople <u>pollute</u> the water and cause the river's fish to die, we are studying geography.

Geographers use the terms **physical geography** to refer to the actual makeup of the land—in our example, the river—and <u>**cultural**</u> **geography** to refer to the study of the people who live and work there—in our case, some of the people who pollute the water.

Geographic facts have always shaped our lives in some way, even if we haven't recognized the connections at first. Specifically, geography affects the political <u>boundaries</u> of our country, the kinds of jobs available for workers, how we move around, who and how many people live near us, the kinds of foods we can buy, their cost, and so on.

Now think of a typical day:

- We wake up and wash, but do we wonder where the water source is located in relation to where we live?
- We look out the window and see mountains in the distance; how long have they been there, and what are their effects on the city's weather?
- We sit down to eat breakfast, made up of foods from all over the world. Why do certain products grow in different locales? How do the foods get to the table? How might the trucks and planes, which deliver them fresh, be polluting the air, making it more difficult to grow these products in the future?
- We listen to the radio or television and hear about events in faraway countries, where people speak languages we can't pronounce, dress in exotic fashions, and live lifestyles far removed from ours.

To think about the world in all these ways is *to think geographically*—in other words, to be interested in, question, and understand how everything in our world is connected.

Humans haven't always been so geographically minded. People who lived ten thousand years ago had little understanding of the world around them; the subject of geography was totally foreign to them. But over time, people became more interested in their own place in the world, as well as places that were farther away but that they had heard of. People began to ask questions:

- Where are we?
- How are people in other places similar to and different from us?
- Why is it so hot here?
- Why does the sun rise in the east and set in the west—every single day, in twenty-four-hour sequences?
- Are there people living on other planets?

EARLY GEOGRAPHY

Indeed, people all over the world were asking questions about Earth. First were the people in ancient Mesopotamia (*meh* suh puh TAY mee uh) in what is present-day Iraq. These people made and used maps as early as four thousand years ago to show the boundaries of cities. In fact, this region produced the first "world map," which showed what these people knew of the world at that point; they may not have known much, but, still, they mapped it out.

At about the same time, another group of people, the Egyptians, were making maps, which appear to have been used to help the government collect taxes. The Chinese, also, were advanced in their mapmaking skills hundreds of years before the birth of Christ; there are written indications that maps were used in China before 700 B.C., but the earliest surviving example is from 200 B.C.; it shows the boundaries between different cities, as well as significant natural landmarks.

The Greeks

The ancient Greeks built on much of this foundation and truly advanced the field of geography. The Greeks were more <u>systematic</u> than earlier examiners and explainers of the physical world around them.

Many people give **Thales** (THAY leez), a Greek man who lived more than twenty-five hundred years ago, the credit for being the first geographer because of his careful observations and explanations of the physical world. To measure distances between places, he devised a system similar to the present system of miles (or kilometers).

In addition to Thales, other early Greek geographers used mathematical skills to calculate the size of Earth and figured out a good deal of accurate information about Earth's climates, particularly near the equator. Then the second-century Egyptian-Greek named **Claudius Ptolemy** (TAHL uh mee) wrote the eight-volume *Geographica,* which laid out the locations, by latitude and longitude, of all known places at that point in history. See Chapter 2 for explanations of how latitude and longitude and the grid system work on maps.

Despite his great contributions, Ptolemy was significantly wrong on one important point: the size of Earth. He accepted an eighteen-thousand-mile (twenty-nine-thousand-kilometer) estimate of the <u>circumference</u> at the equator instead of the correct figure of twenty-five thousand miles (forty thousand kilometers); Columbus used this inaccurate figure in the fifteenth century to convince his backers to let him try his voyage to find Asia by sailing west.

The Romans

The next major advances in geography and **cartography** (the art and science of making maps) took place in the Roman Empire. Rather than the scientific curiosity that fueled the Greeks' investigations, the Romans had a very different <u>motivation</u>: the practical necessities of operating a far-flung empire. They made maps to show the political divisions of their territories, different types of farming in different places, the locations of cities, and the best routes for traveling between them—as we said, very practical uses.

GEOGRAPHY IN EUROPE GOES DARK, BUT ELSEWHERE . . .

Then, in the first few hundred years of the Middle Ages (A.D. 500–1500), the art and science of geography didn't advance much in Europe. Mainly, Europeans of this period produced religiously influenced maps, many of which showed the city Jerusalem in the Holy Land as the center of the universe. These Europeans lost the Greeks' mathematical information about Earth and focused their geographic activity on faith-based but untraceable information. (For example, a lot of energy went into trying to determine the exact location of the Garden of Eden by following references in the first book of the Bible.) For European geography, this was truly a "dark age." Arab cartographers, however, were producing maps that accurately showed much of the then-known world, using Arabic translations of the ancient Greeks' works.

Europeans renewed their interest in geography when the Crusades began in 1099. These were military <u>expeditions</u> undertaken by Christian powers to win the Holy Land, which was in the hands of Muslims. Although their efforts to recapture and hold Jerusalem ultimately failed, the Christians' travels to the east fueled an <u>emerging</u> interest in the rest of the world, for here the Europeans met different people and heard tales of what lay beyond the Holy Land. Over the next few hundred years, a series of scientific, <u>technological</u>, and commercial developments combined to change

Map of the Roman Empire in the time of Constantine

the nature of European geography—and the history of the entire world.

EUROPEANS EXPLORE THE WORLD

The fifteenth century saw tremendous change and showed that geography and history connect in powerful ways. At this time, Ptolemy's *Geographica* was found and translated into Latin, making it available to the population of Europe; then the invention of the printing press, which made quick and inexpensive copies, allowed even more people to read Ptolemy and to study maps.

This era is called the **Age of Exploration** because of the amount of exploring and "discover-

ing" by Europeans at this time. (*Discovering*, of course, is a complicated idea, since many of these "new" lands were new only to the Europeans. However, geographically, this was, indeed, a time of great activity.)

In addition to looking again at Greek writings about the world and making progress in printing, three other factors combined at this time to move geographic knowledge forward: a demand for faster and safer trade routes between Asia and Europe, advances in shipbuilding, and advances in navigational instruments.

A good deal of the credit for wanting to know more about the world goes to **Marco Polo,** an earlier European traveler and geographer, whose book,

Description of the World, written in 1298, became popular now and fired up the imaginations and economic desires of much of Europe. His accounts of the spices and other treasures of China and other parts of the East led to establishing overland trade routes, which could bring these new products to Europe. But these trade routes were slow and expensive. The Europeans wanted to be able to exchange goods with the East by other means and started wondering, can we get there by water?

Traveling by water presented its own huge—and unknown—obstacles of a geographic nature. How could someone establish a trade route through waters that had not been mapped? No one knew exactly what sailors would come across as they ventured far out of sight of Europe's coastlines, particularly in sailing vessels that might not stand up during voyages of thousands of miles. But Polo's accounts had so fanned the flames of interest among Europeans, that some brave individuals pursued the possibilities, despite the dangers.

Prince Henry the Navigator

Prince Henry the Navigator, strange to say, never did much sailing himself; his name came about because of his support of explorers and the navigation school he opened in the southern port of Portugal in the early 1400s. His hope was to develop a water route around Africa so that he could trade with Asia. He organized sailing expeditions south, to explore and chart the coast of Africa, with the goal of eventually navigating all the way around the southern tip of the continent. (Prince Henry also was hoping to discover gold and convert people in other lands to Christianity; much exploration at this time had multiple goals.)

In addition to organizing and financing the actual voyages, Prince Henry was involved in another key development: the construction of the **caravel,** a new and faster sailing ship. This ship used triangular sails, as well as square ones. This arrangement of sails permitted the ship to sail into the wind and so make long-range trips possible. The caravel also had a large hold to store the products the Europeans hoped to transport.

The first concrete proof of the caravel and the soundness of Prince Henry's vision was a sail in 1488 by the Portuguese explorer **Bartolomeu Dias** (DEE uhs) all the way down the western coast of

Caravel (sailing ship)

Africa to the continent's southern tip. Then a <u>decade</u> later, **Vasco da Gama** sailed around Africa's southern tip and all the way to India, achieving Prince Henry's dream of a water route to Asia.

Columbus Does . . . What Exactly?

Despite the tremendous courage it took to sail down the coast of Africa, most of those voyages still took place through waters that were relatively known and that were not very far from the coast. To attempt to reach Asia by sailing in the opposite direction—going west to reach the East—would mean sailing through totally unknown seas. That was the radical idea that Christopher Columbus advanced.

From geographical and historical viewpoints, a great deal of misinformation about Columbus still exists, despite the efforts of the past few decades to clarify some of the most mistaken information that students used to learn.

- First, Columbus did not think, nor did most of the people sailing with him (nor most of literate Europe, for that matter), that he risked falling off the edge of Earth because it was flat; that much of the Greeks' insights had been safeguarded.
- Second, he never reached North America, although he did touch on the mainland of South America and several islands of the Caribbean.
- And, of course, he didn't "discover" these lands, since there were already millions of people living there.

But what Columbus did do was to start a far-reaching encounter between different parts of the world that, until then, had been largely ignorant of the other's existence. After him, many more European explorers and settlers traveled to what became known as the Americas. They brought with them their ideas, food, culture, and diseases and took back many of the same things from the native populations to Europe.

Why Don't We Live in Christophia?

Despite Columbus's accomplishment, he didn't get as much credit in one sense as he might have expected; that is, Europeans did not name this "New World" after him. Rather, a German mapmaker-geographer seems to have named the newly "discovered" land America, after **Amerigo Vespucci** (ves POO chee), an Italian sailor, who made several voyages for Spain between 1497 and 1503; Vespucci was the first European to realize he had come upon a new continent, unlike Columbus and others who thought they had landed in Asia. There is also a new theory that America was named for an English merchant named Amerik.

The interesting geographic mistake mentioned here truly affected Columbus's success. Columbus, accepting the calculation that the world was less than eighteen thousand miles (twenty-nine thousand kilometers) around, had based his supplies and plans on that figure (of course, he was wrong by about a third, but that wasn't his fault!). If he had known Earth really was closer to twenty-five thousand miles (forty thousand kilometers) around, he might never have started in the first place; second, if the "new" continent hadn't been there for him to bump into, he surely would have died before reaching Asia. Sometimes what you don't know can actually help you!

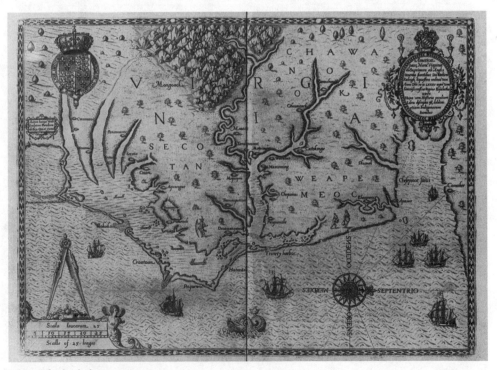

Map of Virginia, 1585

The Role of Technology

In addition to the advances in shipbuilding that made the exploration era possible, developments in navigational techniques and instruments also gave these explorers a better chance of success. Sailors had been using compasses to determine directions for several hundred years, going back to around A.D. 1000, when the Chinese mounted a major sea expedition to India. The Europeans also had used this navigational aid for quite some time before Columbus's voyages; without it, Columbus wouldn't have been able to consider such a long-range attempt.

The Europeans felt bold at this time because of improvements in other navigational devices, including the **astrolabe** and the **sextant,** which helped ships to determine their location at sea. Although such instruments had existed since the ancient Greeks, new, improved ones made longer trips possible. The next major advance in navigational science didn't occur until 1762, when, after a search of many years, a British mathematician, **John Harrison,** developed the No. 4 Marine Chronometer, a clock that could accurately keep time at sea. This tool permitted sailors to calculate accurately their longitude, ending their reliance on the unsafe technique of **dead reckoning,** which used landmarks and astronomical sightings to determine position.

Exploration's End

Prince Henry's efforts on behalf of Portugal and Columbus's voyages began more than four hundred years of exploration and settlement, which ended only in the early twentieth century. At first, the Spanish dominated in South America and Mexico. They were followed in the sixteenth and seventeenth centuries by the British, Dutch, and other European powers, who traveled throughout America and much of Asia. In the 1770s, Britain's **James Cook** was the first European to reach Australia.

Africa was the last major inhabited area to be explored by the Europeans but not until the nineteenth century; before that, they had known little more than the coasts, where they'd been active in the international slave trade and other business pursuits. However, in the 1800s, Europeans ex-

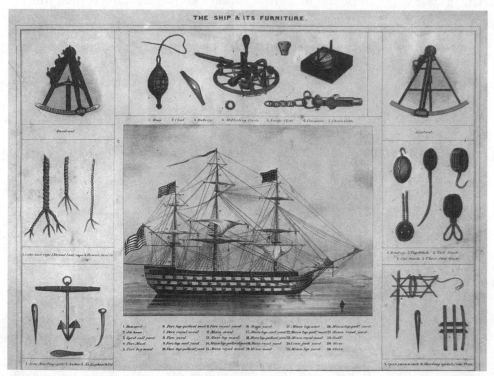

Ship with navigational tools, including quadrant

plored and <u>exploited</u> Africa's interiors. Among the more notable adventurers were **David Livingstone** and **Henry Morton Stanley,** who explored a great deal of the central part of the continent.

This era of exploration came to an end in the early 1900s, when expeditions achieved two goals—reaching the North Pole and reaching the South Pole. **Robert E. Peary** and **Matthew A. Henson,** two Americans, accompanied by four Eskimos, were the first men to reach the North Pole, on April 6, 1909, while **Roald Amundsen** and four others reached the South Pole on December 14, 1911.

HISTORY AND GEOGRAPHY

History is full of examples of the interplay between geography and history; indeed, it's safe to say that geography has had a role in virtually every period of the world's history, from decisions about where

The Portuguese navigator Magellan holding a globe and compass

---

Why Not China or Arabia?

Why was it the Europeans, not the Chinese or the Arabs, who decided to explore more of the unknown world? There were geographic, historical, and cultural reasons that the Chinese and Arabs took a backseat.

By the mid-fifteenth century, the Chinese had already proved they were great sailors: China had sent fleets of more than sixty ships, under the leadership of admiral **Zheng He** (JENG HEE), to develop trade connections with India, Arabia, and the countries of eastern Africa. At least one historian now theorizes that Zheng He reached the New World before Columbus. But China's longer tradition of isolationism won out, and the country stopped He's explorations.

The Arab world had the ability to sail the oceans during the Age of Exploration, because their shipbuilding techniques were as advanced as the Europeans', but they lacked the motivation to go farther; they already had set up functioning trade routes to Asia, which they felt were good enough.

---

to build cities to the outcomes of famous battles. Thousands of examples exist.

Let's begin by examining how physical geography has influenced the location of cities and towns and the borders between countries. A number of different physical factors contributed to the rise of population centers in specific places. Water is perhaps the most important factor: cities were built alongside important rivers and lakes and next to ports and harbors. These sites provided inhabitants with a series of advantages: natural defense, a means of traveling to other places, a way to transport goods for trade, and a supply of water for a variety of needs. Water in the form of rainfall is also an aspect of geography that affects population centers; without adequate rain, people can't live for long in one area.

Mountains and hills also determine where cities and towns grow. Many European cities were situated on hilltops to provide them with a natural form of defense.

Finally, the political boundaries of many nations are formed by natural boundaries: mountains and rivers. The border between the United States and Mexico is the Rio Grande River, Spain and France are divided by the Pyrenees Mountains, the Carpathian Mountains divide several eastern European countries from each other, and the Himalayas serve the same function in south-central Asia.

Geography's Role in World Events

Even more than determining where people lived, geography has been an important element of so much of what has happened in history. Here are a few examples.

- In 2001, the United States did not start bombing Taliban sites in Afghanistan until the president was sure of support from neighboring Pakistan.
- In 1991, the United States and other countries went to war with Iraq in Operation Desert Storm for a variety of reasons—one of the most critical being the vast quantities of oil in the area. If not for the oil resources, the short war might never have taken place.
- Weather is part of geography, and during World War II the Germans failed in their invasion of Russia to a large extent because of terrible weather, particularly during the decisive battles of Moscow and Stalingrad.
- The fateful decision to launch the successful Allied invasion of France on June 6, 1944, was delayed until the last moment while the military leaders waited for the most up-to-the-minute weather report, which gave them a window of opportunity to launch their attack before bad weather reappeared.
- Panama became an independent country by breaking away from Colombia in 1903, in part because the United States wanted to build a canal in Panama between the Atlantic and the Pacific oceans. (Colombia had refused American requests to build the canal, so the United

States offered naval support to the independence drive of the Panamanian revolutionaries.) The Panama Canal, completed in 1914, made it possible to avoid the long trek around the tip of South America.

- **Napoleon** had wanted to conquer all of Europe in the early nineteenth century, but his mission <u>foundered</u> also because of bad weather in Russia. His troops froze to death because of the horrific winter storm conditions that descended on them.
- Geography played a role in isolating some societies from others, as we've already seen in the example of China sealing itself off from other countries with the Great Wall. Japan, too, once relied on its physical characteristics to develop in isolation. The archipelago and its mountainous land helped to serve the political goals of the **shoguns,** the powerful military rulers of Japan, who dominated the society from 1192 to 1868. After their fall, Japan began an <u>accelerated</u> program of contact with other countries, which greatly changed its political, technological, and financial development.
- In one of the most famous early (218 B.C.) examples of overcoming geography, **Hannibal,** a general of Carthage in North Africa, crossed the seemingly impassable Alps between France and Italy in fifteen days, using elephants; he achieved surprise and defeated the Romans.

Geography's Role in U.S. History

Much of American history is also linked to geography.

- The choice of key sites for principal American cities during the colonial period had to do with location: Boston, New York, Philadelphia, and Charleston all became leading trading centers because of their natural harbors.
- Furthermore, the Allegheny Mountains limited expansion westward for much of this period.
- Philadelphia was chosen as the site for writing the Declaration of Independence because of its centrality in the thirteen colonies (it was also the biggest population center at the time).

- Some of the most recognizable lines of the most famous poem about the American Revolution—"Paul Revere's Ride," by Henry Wadsworth Longfellow—focus on geography. Revere's lantern signals to his fellow rebels depended on which route the British took when leaving Boston to attack at Lexington and Concord: "One if by land, and two if by sea, and I on the opposite shore shall be. . . ."

- The territorial expansion of the United States from thirteen states on the east coast to a nation of fifty states spanning the continent (and beyond) took place through force and through purchase, but the most dramatic growth occurred with the Louisiana Purchase. The land that President Thomas Jefferson bought from Napoleon in 1803 doubled the size of the United States and gave it a vast area rich in resources. Geography also played a role in Napoleon's decision to sell: France was involved in a costly land-and-sea war with the British. He needed more funds for his troops, and he believed that Louisiana was too far from France to hold on to.

- The outcome of one of the most decisive battles of the Civil War, Gettysburg, hinged on which of the two opposing armies could occupy the little town's high ground in the early stages of fighting. Because of the foresight of one Union general, the North got there first and held on for three days, to turn the tide of the war in its favor.

- Indeed, the outcome of the Civil War itself was a function of geography: while the South had mostly agricultural plantations, the North had many more industrial factories in urban centers, giving the Union a tremendous advantage in the construction of war materials.

- The separation of the United States from Europe and Asia by oceans shaped the American role, to some extent, in both world wars. We entered both conflicts only after they had been raging for several years. In the early stages, we served as the "arsenal of democracy" before sending our own troops to engage directly in combat. Our amazing economic success in the twentieth century was spurred by the lack of physical destruction here, while so much of the rest of the developed world was destroyed and had to be rebuilt. (Technology, however, can trump geography: weapons can now span the oceans.)

- Geography's role in American history becomes clear if we examine the names of some of our most popular sports teams: the Pittsburgh *Steelers*, because the city's location at the junction of three rivers made it an ideal site for its steel mills in the late nineteenth century; the Chicago *Bulls*, because of the city's focus as a meatpacking center, the destination of cattle raised in the Southwest; the Portland *Trailblazers*, because Americans had to cut their own trails across the country in the expansion from east to west; and the Los Angeles *Lakers*, not because there are so many lakes in L.A., but because the team formerly was in Minneapolis, Minnesota, the "land of a thousand lakes."

GEOGRAPHY IN THE TWENTY-FIRST CENTURY

Despite the fact that the world has been fully explored and mapped, geography still plays a vital role in our modern lives; in many ways, it is as relevant today as ever. Satellites and computers have refined the science of cartography and taken it to new levels. Aerial photography and radar have allowed geographers to determine the exact shape, size, and location of land masses—and landforms under the sea.

Furthermore, satellite transmissions play a role in much of our daily life: constant meteorological updates help us plan outings; cars use a **global positioning system (GPS)** to help us with phone calls and directions; golfers benefit from carts equipped with advanced technology that can tell the distance between a player's position in the fairway and the pin on the green.

! Implications

To answer the question, "Why does all this matter?" or "What does it mean?," share the following insights with your child.

Geography has played—and still plays—an essential role in much of human life. Ancient Greeks first started to arrange facts about the world around them; in the eighteenth and nineteenth centuries, geography became a separate field of study; now, modern technology keeps telling us more about the world.

Being able *to think geographically* adds meaning to our lives. It can help us to understand other people and their cultures, providing insights about why people dress, eat, think, work, worship, and travel differently from us. In addition, knowing about geography can help us figure out how to get there if we become intrigued enough to want to go see a place for ourselves.

A grasp of geography's role in history is critical to being able to understand why things happened the way they did and can help us interpret the news we read and see everyday. Without the skills and insights of geographers, our cities, roads, airports, and other physical sites wouldn't be as well designed or constructed.

Geography is one of the key factors in the distribution of wealth around the world, playing a role in the relative wealth and poverty of different nations. We need to be able to see the role that it has played in the development of different societies.

We live in an era of heightened connectivity, spending much of our lives interacting, directly and indirectly, with people who live thousands of miles away: through the Internet, business connections, travel, international media links, and so on. Just as people wanted to go out exploring the unknown world for thousands of years, we can use our modern technology and increased understanding of the world's geography to enable us to explore and discover more of our world's riches and diversity.

✓ Fact Checker

To check that your child knows or can find the basic facts in this chapter, here is a puzzle based on names of people and places discussed.

GEOGRAPHY PUZZLE

Use the clues to complete the following puzzle. Write one letter of each answer on a blank line. The letters in the vertical rectangle spell the name of an early geographer.

1. The people who lived here made maps four thousand years ago.
2. This ancient Greek is called the first geographer.
3. This word means "the art and science of making maps."
4. This man was the first to sail down the west coast of Africa and on to India.
5. Prince Henry the Navigator came from this country.
6. This man thought Earth measured only eighteen thousand miles around.
7. The "New World" is named for this man.
8. The late 1400s and the early 1500s are called the Age of _____.
9. This is a basic navigation tool.

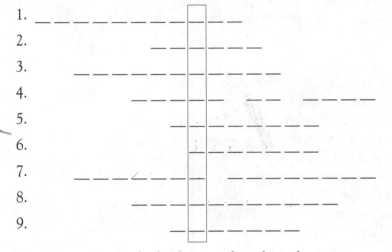

Answers appear in the back, preceding the index.

? The Big Questions

The following questions encourage your child to think critically rather than simply recall facts. If necessary, review the specific information from the preceding pages that will help your child make the appropriate inferences to come up with reasonable answers.

1. What do people mean when they say that improved communications such as the telephone and the Internet make the world both smaller *and* larger?
2. What roles has the natural resource water played for humans during the last four thousand years?
3. Review the developments, discussed in the chapter, in understanding geography. Which one or two do you consider most important? Why?

Possible Answers

1. Improved communications can bring people and nations closer and in that way can make the world smaller. At the same time, improved communications can expand an individual's understanding and in that way can make the individual's world larger.

2. Water, often in the form of rivers, has been necessary for agriculture, for trade, and for exploration.

3. Accept any answer that the child can support with details from the chapter.

Skills Practice

The following activities give your child practice in applying the skills basic to social studies. For some of the activities, your child may need to review the information in the preceding pages.

A. LEARNING FROM PRIMARY SOURCES

Either read to your child or ask your child to read this passage about October 12 and October 13, 1492. Christopher Columbus wrote the passage in the ship's log. The American poet William Carlos Williams translated it into English. (See In the American Grain, New Directions, 1925.) Ask your child to read or listen carefully so that he or she can figure out from this passage what Columbus thought of the people he met.

On Friday, the twelfth of October, we anchored before the land and made ready to go on shore. Presently we saw naked people on the beach. I went ashore in the armed boat. . . . And we saw the trees very green, and much water and fruits of diverse kinds. Presently many of the inhabitants assembled. I gave to some red caps and glass beads to put round their necks, and many other things of little value. They came to the ships' boats afterward, where we were, swimming and bringing us parrots, cotton threads in skeins, darts—what they had, with good will. . . .

On Saturday, as dawn broke, many of these people came to the beach, all youths [young men]. Their legs are very straight, all in one line and no belly. They came to the ship in canoes, made out of the trunk of a tree, all in one piece, and wonderfully worked, propelled with a paddle like a baker's shovel, and go at a marvelous speed.

Question

What do you think Columbus thought about the people he found where he landed? What do you think the natives may have thought of Columbus?

Possible Answers

- *Columbus went ashore in an armed boat. He may have thought that he would need protection from the people he saw on land.*
- *Then Columbus gave the people cheap gifts. He may not have respected the people very much.*
- *Columbus describes the young men's bodies. It seems that he thought the young men looked healthy.*
- *Columbus describes the canoes. It seems that he admired them.*
- *The natives seemed friendly toward Columbus. They brought gifts. They didn't seem to have weapons with them.*

Evaluating Your Child's Skills: In order to answer the question successfully, your child will need to go beyond specific information to make inferences. If your child has trouble with this skill, demonstrate for him or her how you would arrive at one of the answers. Talk through your own thought process. For example, you might point to the third sentence in the passage and say, "I see here that Columbus went ashore in an armed boat. Why did he mention that the boat was armed? He must have thought that there was a possibility that the native people would be hostile."

B. FROM SPECIFICS TO GENERALIZATION

Make your child conscious of how dependent many of us are on the rest of the world by suggesting that he or she conduct the following inventory.

For one day, list every product you use at home—food, clothes, soap, appliances, and so on. Next to each item on the list, note the city, state, or country where it grew or was processed or manufactured. At the end of the day, you will have a list of specific pieces of information.

Your next task will be to write a general statement—a generalization—that grows out of the individual specifics. For example, one person might write, "More than half the items I use every day are from Japan," while another might write, "My food is from all over the world, but all my clothes come from the U.S.A."

Evaluating Your Child's Skills: In order to complete this task successfully, your child will have to keep clear records and then analyze the facts to write a general statement that is neither too narrow nor too broad. If your child has trouble with this task, show him or her how to set up paper or a computer screen for record keeping. Then ask your child questions such as, "Do most of the things you use at home come from this country or from other countries?"

C. CLASSIFYING EVENTS ON A TIMELINE

Ask the following question to help your child work with a timeline.

According to this timeline, what do the events on the following dates have in common: 1488, 1522, 1607, 1903, 1969?

1488	Dias is the first to sail around the tip of Africa.
1518	European diseases begin to kill natives in the New World.
1522	Magellan's crew completes the first trip around the world.
1543	Copernicus claims Earth revolves around the sun.
1607	English establish the first permanent colony in America.
1803	United States makes Louisiana Purchase.
1903	Wright brothers make the first successful airplane flight.
1969	Human walks on the moon for the first time.

Suggested Answer

Each of the dates marks a "first" by humans in overcoming a difficulty or problem posed by geography.

Evaluating Your Child's Skills: In order to succeed with this activity, your child needs to read the timeline items closely and infer how events are similar. Reinforce your child's scanning and skimming skills by suggesting that he or she look for the word *first* on the items on the timeline.

☆ # Top of the Class

Children interested in delving more deeply into the topics covered in this chapter can choose one or more of the following activities. They may do the activities for their own satisfaction or report in class on what they have done to show that they have been seriously considering the history of geography.

SPEAKING OF GREEK: WORD BUILDING

Your child has learned that the word *geography* comes from two Greek word parts: *geo,* meaning "earth," and *graph,* meaning "writing." Now work with other Greek word parts so that your child can do more word building.

Here are some Greek word parts and their translations. Put these word parts with *graph* to make English words that have something to do with writing. Be sure you can define each word you list. You might hold a contest with friends or classmates to see who can list the most English words about writing using *graph.* You can use more than one form of a word—for example, both *biography* and *biographical.*

auto = self	*bio* = life
photo = light	*biblio* = book
tele = far away	

BOOKS TO READ AND RECOMMEND IN CLASS

Suggest that your child read one of the following titles and tell why the book did or did not appeal to him or her. Your child might think about whether he or she would have liked to take the trip described in the book.

Columbus, Christopher. *The Log of Christopher Columbus' First Voyage to America in the year 1492 as Copied Out in Brief by Bartholomew Las Casas.* Little, Brown, 1989.

Greene, Carol. *Marco Polo: Voyager to the Orient.* Children's Press, 1987.

Humble, Richard. *The Voyage of Magellan.* Watts, 1989.

Osborne, Mary Pope. *The Story of Christopher Columbus, Admiral of the Ocean Sea.* Dell, 1987.

MAKING A COMPASS

This chapter explains that compasses were necessary to guide explorers in the past. Of course, they still are. Help your child make a simple compass to figure out which direction is north and, by extension, where south, east, and west are.

Materials

saucer or bowl of water	rectangular slice of cork
magnet with labeled poles	transparent tape
	needle

Method

1. Place just enough water in the bowl for the slice of cork to float.
2. Hold the needle by the eye, and stroke it about thirty times with one pole of the magnet. Stroke in *one* direction only.
3. Tape the magnetized needle to the top of the cork.
4. Float the cork and needle in the water. Does one end of the needle indeed point north? You may know which way is north, or you can

verify which direction is north by using a store-bought compass.

5. Let your child gently turn the rectangle of cork to see that the needle will seek out north and make the cork turn back to its original position.

6. You may choose to offer an explanation now for the needle's behavior: the North and South poles of Earth are poles of a magnet, and opposite poles of a magnet attract each other, so every magnet (including the magnetized needle), if allowed to float or swing freely, will align itself with one end pointing to Earth's North Pole. Or you may want to hold this explanation of magnetic poles until a later chapter.

CHAPTER 2

Understanding Maps and Globes

The globe pictured here is only one of many ways to represent the world. This chapter explores various methods, pointing out their advantages and disadvantages.

Double stereopticon photo of the Gigantic Globe, Paris Exposition 1900

Word Power

Word	Definition
climate	usual weather in a place
distortion	incorrect representation
distribution	spreading out
dynasties	families or groups that rule or govern a country for a long time without interruption
hydroelectric	related to production of electricity by water power
migrations	movements of people from one location to another
minerals	natural substances that are not animals or plants—for example, gold, salt, copper
nuclear	related to power created by smashing atoms
oriented	adjusted; clear in one's thinking about what one is looking at
parallel	two straight lines in the same direction that never meet
proportion	relationship in size of one thing to another
provinces	administrative or political regions of a country, much like states of the United States
sphere	solid shape like a basketball
temperate	moderate in terms of climate, with neither extreme of hot or cold
tropical	related to the area between the tropics of Capricorn and Cancer, characterized by high temperatures and humidity

What Your Child Needs to Know

You may choose to use the following text in several different ways, depending on your child's strengths and preferences. You might read the passage aloud; you might read it to yourself and then paraphrase it for your child; or you might ask your child to read the material along with you or on his or her own.

INTRODUCTION TO MAPS AND GLOBES

Now that we know what geography is and why people have been so interested in it for the past several thousand years, let's examine the tools and techniques that geographers have developed to represent Earth and its parts. The two general tools geographers use are globes and maps.

One of the great things about living in the early twenty-first century is that we can actually see pictures from space that show the size and shape of Earth. But more than twenty-five hundred years ago, the ancient Greeks were able to figure out these two important geographical facts without the benefit of photography; instead, they relied on their powers of observation and their mathematical skills to construct the first globes in history.

GLOBES

A globe is the most accurate way to represent Earth because a globe is a sphere—and Earth is roughly a sphere. A globe can show all of the continents and oceans in their correct positions and, more significant, in correct proportion so that you can tell how big one place is compared to another or how far it is from one city to another.

Most globes use certain techniques and practices to illustrate the major parts of Earth; for example, usually, a globe is mostly blue: that color represents all the oceans and lakes in the world. The other significant areas on the globe—continents, countries, mountains, deserts, forests—appear in other colors.

LATITUDE AND LONGITUDE

The series of lines running horizontally and vertically around the globe (see the illustration at the beginning of this chapter) are important markings that help geographers, explorers, and travelers figure out where they are in the world. The markings on the globe (they do not exist in the real world) make it possible for people to go out exploring or to sail their boats from one island to another far off the coast of the United States with the full knowledge and confidence of being able to get where they intend to go and of returning.

The imaginary parallel lines circling Earth horizontally are called lines of latitude, and they tell how far north or how far south a place is from the **equator,** the center line of latitude, which is zero degrees latitude (written as 0°). The equator, in other words, is the starting point for measuring latitude. The North Pole is ninety degrees north latitude (written as 90° N), and the South Pole is ninety degrees south latitude (90° S); these are the farthest north and farthest south points on Earth. Every place in between is a certain parallel; they never meet. These lines do get progressively shorter as they approach either pole.

Longitude is shown by a series of lines called **meridians** that run north and south from one pole to the other. Unlike lines of latitude, they aren't parallel; rather, they do meet at each pole. These lines tell how far east or how far west a place is from the prime meridian, which was designated zero degrees longitude (written as 0°) and runs through Greenwich, England. The world is divided into two sections, from 0 degrees to 179 degrees east longitude (170° E) and from 0 degrees to 179 degrees west longitude (179° W).

A degree of latitude or longitude is divided into sixty minutes (shown with a ′), which are further divided into seconds (shown with a ″). All of these markings form a geographic grid on the globe, allowing us to identify our precise location in relation to the equator and the prime meridian. For example, we can say, "Our location is 23°20′ N, 145°19′ E." Anyone else with a globe can then find us. (Anyone with the right map can also find us; more about maps follows.)

Each degree of latitude represents about 69 miles (111 kilometers). The distance between two degrees of longitude varies, depending on distance from the equator; the distances get smaller as one moves away from the equator, reaching zero at the poles.

Latitude and longitude also are useful for separating Earth into four different hemispheres: northern, southern, eastern, and western. The equator divides Earth into Northern and Southern hemispheres; the prime meridian divides Earth into the Eastern hemisphere (from 0° to 179° E) and the Western hemisphere (from 0° to 179° W). (See the pictures of hemispheres at the beginning of Chapter 7.)

The globe has two other key latitude lines, which serve to separate different <u>climate</u> zones. The tropic of Cancer, at 23°30′ N, divides the Northern Hemisphere into a <u>tropical</u> zone (from the equator to the tropic of Cancer) and a <u>temperate</u> zone, extending from the tropic of Cancer to the Arctic Circle (66°30′ N). The tropic of Capricorn, at 23°30′ S, does the same for the Southern Hemisphere: a tropical zone runs between it and the equator, while a temperate zone ranges south from the tropic of Capricorn to the Antarctic Circle, at 66°30′ S. (For the positions of the two imaginary tropic lines, see page 51, which illustrates the connection between the revolution of Earth and seasons.)

Place versus Location

Geographers use the word *place* when they are describing the physical and human characteristics of a site such as a mountain or a river or a city—the types of animals and people who live there, the kinds of buildings people have constructed, and the structure of their government. We say, for example, "The *place* I'd most like to visit is Mexico City, one of the highest cities in the world."

The word *location,* on the other hand, refers to the specific position of a point on Earth. There are two ways to express location: absolute location is expressed in terms of latitude and longitude. We say, "The location of Mexico City is 19° N latitude and 90° W longitude." Relative location explains where a point is in relation to another point. We say, "New York is south of Boston," for example.

MAPS

Now that we've explained globes, we need to add an important cautionary note. Globes have two big drawbacks. First, they're hard to carry around in a book bag or to print inside a textbook. Second, they're relatively small, so they can't contain a lot of details. These are the reasons that cartography—defined in Chapter 1 as "the art and science of making maps"—developed.

Cartography has been in existence for thousands of years, even though no one knows for sure who made the first maps or what they represented. Most probably, they were sketches drawn in the dirt so that one person could show someone else something about where he or she lived. As noted in Chapter 1, the ancient Greeks usually get the credit for developing scientific cartography, even though people in Mesopotamia (which is where modern-day Iraq is located) and in China were extremely good at drawing maps.

Maps can range from a simple sketch representing what a room looks like from above to a detailed illustration of the continents and oceans of Earth; maps can show how many people live in each state of the United States or the dates of battles in the Civil War. In short, people use maps for many varied purposes; think of weather maps, road maps, maps of the mall, voting-pattern maps, and so on. Maps are portable, are easily reproduced in books, can show a lot of detail in a small space, and are easy to store at home or in school.

Projection

As with globes, however, there is a major downside to maps: because they're flat, they can't give a totally accurate picture of Earth. To understand this problem, think of peeling an orange and then trying to paste the rind on a flat piece of paper. Or look at this picture of the peeled surface of a globe; to flatten it, parts of it have been either stretched or cut. There is no way a flat map representation of Earth can do what a globe does: accurately represent the size, shape, and distance of all the different parts in relation to one another. All maps have some kind and level of <u>distortion</u> in them; the bigger the area that is shown, the larger the distortion.

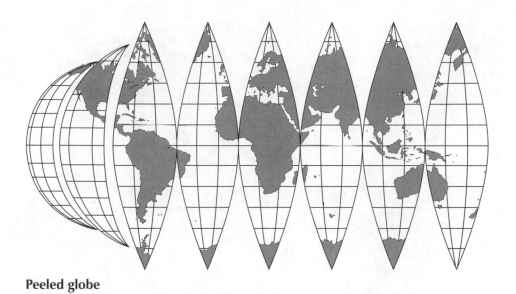

Peeled globe

Projection is the term that cartographers use for the process of taking the globe's accurate information and putting it on a map as realistically as possible. (It's called projection because one way to complete this process is to put a light source inside a globe and *project* its lines of latitude and longitude, as well as the continents and oceans, onto a flat surface, copying them there. The areas farthest from the light source will be the most distorted.) When people make maps today, they don't need to do a physical projection of the globe; rather, they can use mathematical calculations to reconstruct the geographic grid on paper.

There are many different types of map projections; each has its strengths and weaknesses, and the projection chosen for a particular map depends on the type and purpose of the map. We will look at five important ones: Robinson, Goode's Interrupted, Mercator, polar, and conic.

The **Robinson** projection appears in many textbooks because it accurately shows the size and shape of the continents; however, the size of

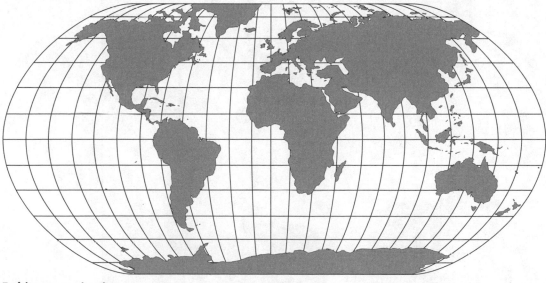

Robinson projection

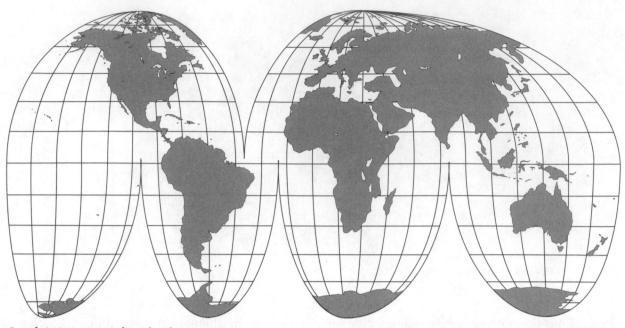

Goode's Interrupted projection

the oceans is expanded somewhat, and the areas closest to the North and South poles are more distorted.

Goode's Interrupted projection does a good job of showing the shapes and sizes of the conti-nents and oceans (it's also called an *equal-area projection* for this reason), but the distances be-tween places are less accurate, particularly in the oceans (notice the cutouts between different parts of the oceans). This type of projection is

Mercator projection

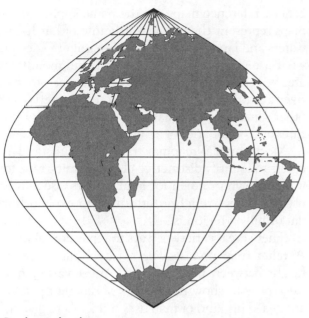

Conic projection

particularly useful for comparing different aspects of the continents.

The **Mercator** projection dates back to 1569, when cartographer **Gerardus Mercator** developed it. It accurately shows the shapes of continents but not their sizes or distances; most significant, areas near the poles are greatly distorted, so that Greenland, for example, appears larger than all of South

America, when it's really only about the size of Mexico. However, because the lines of latitude and longitude are straight on this map, it shows true directions and, therefore, greatly helps people needing a map to navigate at sea.

Conic projections are used mostly for showing one specific area of Earth without much distortion of size, shape, or distance, particularly in the midlatitude areas; for example, if you wanted to depict Europe by itself, a conic projection would be a good choice.

Polar projections represent distance and direction accurately but distort size and shape at the edges. They are good for showing one hemisphere at a time and are favored by pilots, who use them to chart **great circle routes,** which show the shortest path between two points on Earth's surface.

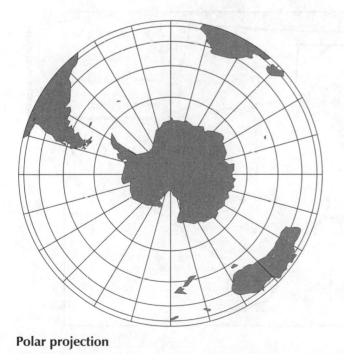

Polar projection

Type of Projection	Description/Strengths/Weaknesses
Robinson (also called oval)	accurate depiction of continents' sizes and shapes; distortion greatest at the poles
Goode's Interrupted	equal-area projection showing sizes and shapes of continents accurately but distorts distances
Mercator (also called cylindrical)	good for navigation at sea because of straight latitude and longitude lines but distorts sizes greatly near the poles
Conic	best for showing one section of Earth without much distortion, especially for midlatitudes
Polar (also called azimuthal)	used mostly to show one hemisphere at a time; accurate for distance and direction; used by pilots for great circle routes

General Reference Maps

People use different maps for different purposes. In general, geographers divide maps into two broad categories: general reference maps and special-purpose, or thematic, maps. Two of the most important general reference maps are political and physical maps.

Political maps represent how humans have divided up the continents, countries, and other places. The markings on these maps show boundaries between countries, locations of principal cities, subdivisions into states, <u>provinces</u>, or districts, and other important information for understanding the political structure of Earth.

These markings, of course, don't really exist, and political maps are being redrawn all of the time, whenever changes occur in political structures around the world. For example, a map from 1985 will show the Soviet Union; a map published today shows no Soviet Union but many different countries and configurations in that part of the world. Given such changes, it's a good idea to make sure any political map that you're using is up-to-date. There's one major exception: if you want to examine the history of a region, older maps are ideal and helpful.

Physical maps are the other major category of general reference maps. As the name implies, these maps represent the physical structure of Earth—its waters and land formations. A physical map depicts what a region looks like: how high the mountains are; how rugged the land is; the presence of lakes, rivers, or other bodies of water, forests, deserts, and other significant information about the natural features and boundaries of an area.

Most physical mapmakers use certain standard colors to identify distinctive physical traits: blue for water, brown or green for land. Colors also can be used to depict **relief,** a term used to explain how flat or hilly a region is.

There are a variety of ways to represent hilliness. A **relief map** uses *shading* to show differences in height between parts of land. An **elevation map** uses *colors* to show the heights of different parts of an area. This kind of map uses numerals to give actual distances above and below sea level. A **contour map** uses lines of different widths to show the different heights, or each contour line shows a step higher or lower of elevation. Where the contour lines are very close together, the land is high, while far-apart lines show flat or gradually rising land. These contour maps are very important for people who like to hike and bike—think about it!

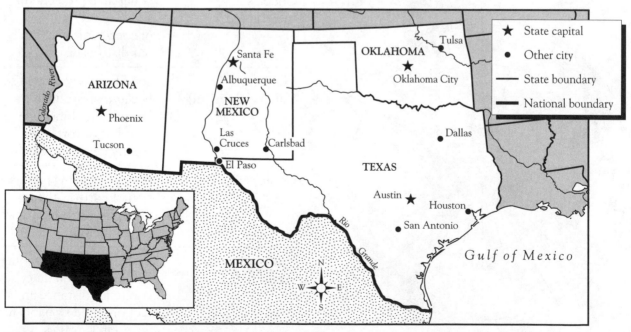

Southwest: political map

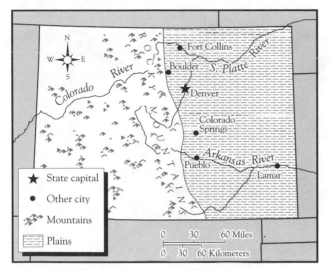

Colorado: physical map

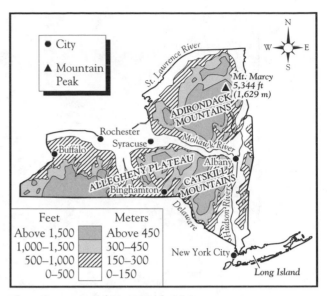

Elevation map of New York State

Special-Purpose Maps

In addition to general reference maps, mapmakers create maps for many specific projects and needs of people. Imagine some specific type of information that might be represented symbolically on a map—and the map probably exists. Some special-purpose maps are of interest to only a small number of people—such as a map of a mall, showing the location of all the stores that are there—while others show information that people all over the world can use—population density in different countries in the world, for example. Some common special-

purpose maps are discussed here; of course, there are many others.

Historical maps help people understand important events from the past, such as battles, explorations, <u>migrations</u>, and the rise and fall of empires and <u>dynasties</u>. The title of the map tells what period of history it is about. We use historical maps to understand how things have changed over time, to find specific details about an important battle or other event, or to understand the past political or cultural structure of a country or region.

Geological maps show the structure of Earth; some may show how Earth formed over the course of millions of years. These maps may contain information about volcanoes, mountains, depths of oceans or lakes, lengths of rivers, and so on. They are extremely important to people who travel in remote areas (through which earlier brave explorers traveled in order to map the region) and to officials, responsible for people's health and safety, who must be aware of what is happening *below* the surface of land and water.

Resource maps contain information about the use of land in different areas. For example, they may show the **natural resources** in an area, such as coal, oil, diamonds, and other <u>minerals</u>; they may show the locations of <u>nuclear</u> or <u>hydroelectric</u> power plants; they may highlight the types of farms in a certain region. Resource maps are important to everyone from government officials to business

Relief map of New York State

29

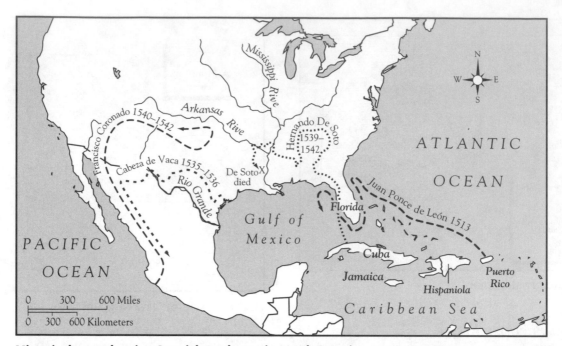

Historical map showing Spanish explorers in North America, 1513–1542

people. For example, people who are planning to build a factory might consult resource maps that show the natural resources, railroads, other factories, and other relevant information in the area they are considering for their project.

Road maps contain information to help people get from one place to another: cities and towns, names and numbers of roads and highways, distances between places, places of interest to see along the way, rest stops, and other helpful facts.

Population maps may show the total number of people living in a specific area. **Population-density maps** are a specific type of population map. They represent the number of people who live in a square mile and so tell us about the <u>distribution</u> of the population—where the most people live and which areas have few people inhabiting them.

Weather maps are familiar to almost all of us from daily newspapers and television reports. They represent the pattern of the weather in a specific region for a fixed period of time. They use specialized shapes and colors to explain what is occurring with the weather in a particular area. **Climate maps** show a different aspect of the weather: they represent a summary of an area's rain, snow, and temperature information for a year.

Vegetation maps represent the types of plants and trees that grow in an area or the type of farming that is taking place.

One last type of special-purpose map is worth noting, and it's one that we don't see represented in books: **mental maps,** which we keep in our heads to represent familiar areas or places. Our earliest and simplest mental maps are usually those of our rooms and homes. From there, we might move on to our immediate neighborhood or town. Anytime you can put places together and represent their relationship to each other in your head, you are creating a mental map. We use mental maps to think about where our homes are in relation to our schools and offices

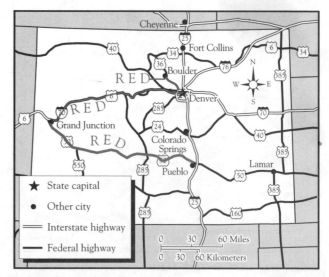

Colorado road map

30

and to think about where the United States is in relation to Canada and Mexico, for example.

Parts of Maps

This section covers what a user needs to know in order to read and understand any map he or she encounters.

Just like a book, every map has a title to tell its readers what it is about. For example, a historical map about significant fighting in the Civil War might have the title "Major Battles of the American Civil War." Looking at the title first is a quick way to get a sense of the information contained in a particular map and whether it's going to be of interest or help.

Usually, off to one side of a map, there's a box known as the **legend,** or **key,** which contains important information, in the form of **symbols,** about the particular markings on that map. For example, some maps identify a capital city with a star or bold letters, while another city may get only a dot. Larger roads on a road map get thicker lines.

As noted, different colors signal elevation, population density, or other information that the map is communicating. For example, maps that were designed to tell about the products made in a region may include pictures to represent the goods.

Often, close to the legend is the map's **scale,** which explains how much a distance on the map is equal to in the real world. For example, a map's scale may indicate that one inch on the map equals a hundred miles on Earth. Thus, if two cities are three inches apart on the map, they are actually three hundred miles apart from each other.

Scale differs from map to map, so it's important to check it on each map. To provide detailed information about a place, a map will use a small scale (see "Map A, India"); to show a greater area but less detail, a map will use a large scale (see "Map B, India"). Anyone who wants to compare two areas—let's say, the state of New York and the country of

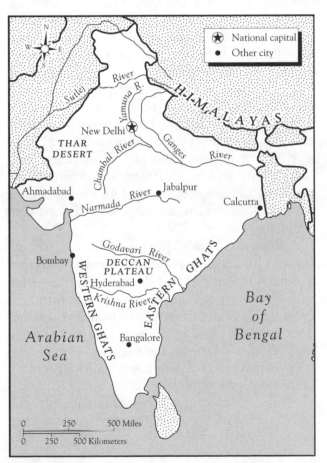

Map A, India

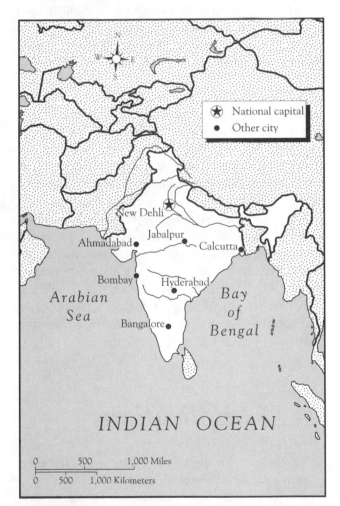

Map B, India

Switzerland—on two different maps must be aware of each map's scale, or the person may come to wrong conclusions.

A map also helps a user to get <u>oriented</u> in terms of direction by building in a **direction marker,** usually an arrow of some sort, which shows the **cardinal directions** on the map: north, south, east, and west. In general, maps show north on the top, south on the bottom, west on the viewer's left, and east on the viewer's right. (Note the directional markers on the two maps of India.)

Sometimes, the directions are noted in a **compass rose,** a fancier kind of directional device, which may also indicate **intermediate directions,** which are halfway between the cardinal directions. For example, northeast (NE) is located halfway between north and east, while southwest (SW) is halfway between south and west.

There are two other features that help users locate places on a map: **coordinates** and a **map grid.** The term *coordinates*, in addition to referring to latitude and longitude, as explained earlier in the chapter, is also the name given to the intersections of lines drawn from numbers and letters around the edges of a map. For example, an alphabetical list of cities on the map may say that such-and-such a city is located at M-7; to find it, the user sees where lines drawn from M and from 7 would intersect, or cross. The map grid is the full set of lines that is drawn from the numbers and letters in the margins of the map to help readers find specific locations.

Finally, some maps include a smaller map, often set off in a box, within the main map. This is an **indicator map,** which helps a user figure out where the subject of the main map is in relation to a larger area. The map called "Southwest: political map," earlier in this chapter, includes an indicator map of the United States to show where the Southwest is in relation to the entire country.

! *Implications*

To answer the question, "Why does all this matter?" or "What does it mean?," share the following insights with your child.

For over twenty-five hundred years, geographers and cartographers have been making maps and globes to represent the world around us to help us find and understand our place in the world. Thousands of maps have been made to serve many different purposes; in fact, there are so many maps available, with so much information in them, that it may seem a little overwhelming.

But reading a map can be just like reading a book. As with learning to read a book, learning to read a map is a specialized skill, which improves with practice.

Maps are similar to books, newspapers, and the evening news in that they all have a *viewpoint*—an *opinion.* You may be somewhat doubtful of this at first, but consider for a moment how cartographers decide where to locate things on a map. Why is it that almost all our maps of the world show the Northern Hemisphere on top? Why is the United States or Europe almost always in the center of the maps?

The answers have a lot to do with politics and power in the world and very little to do with the structure of the physical Earth. In other words, if geography is literally the "writing of the earth" (see Chapter 1), then all maps contain the writer's point of view. For example, each of the different kinds of projections has strengths and weaknesses, and each emphasizes different things.

Even more striking is how different the world can look if it's represented in a new and unusual way on a map; just examine the map here that shows North and South America in different relationships from what we're used to. Understanding what's in—and behind—maps can change your worldview.

Of course, here's the question that still remains: why is it so important to know how to read a map in the first place? That's a good question with many answers. In the past, people turned to geographers and cartographers to help them understand their place in the world, at a time when they actually *weren't sure* where they were in relation to other places. It was comforting for people to know where they stood.

Today, we know our location, so maps play different roles in our lives. On the most practical level, map reading can help us get from place to place without getting lost; it can save us time; and it can

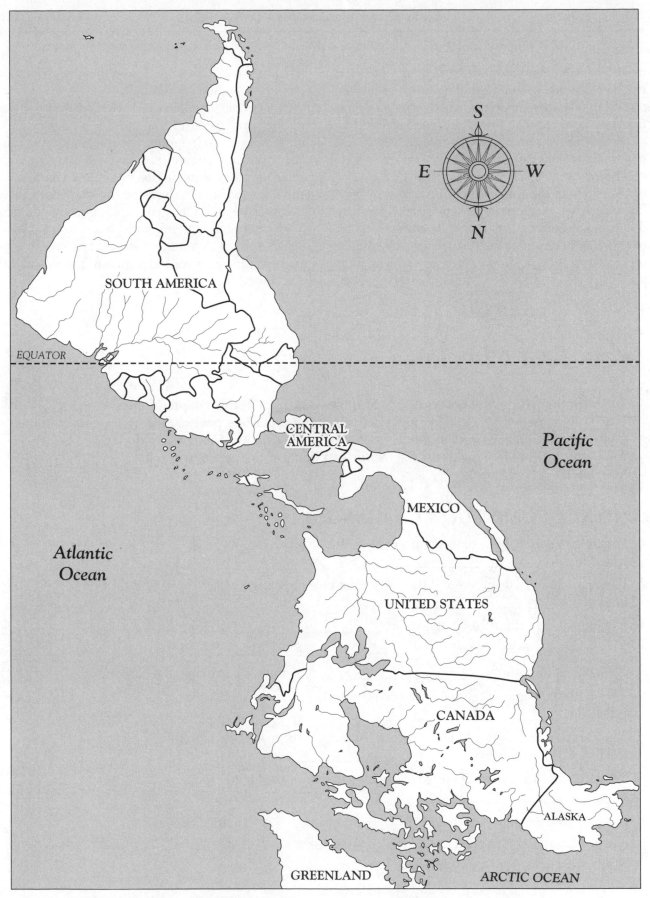

Map showing South America above North America

make our trip more enjoyable by helping us to plan the best possible route, depending on what our interests are. Time is important, whether we are going from our house to the movies or around the world.

For people who are somewhat more adventurous, map-reading skills can be literally life saving. No serious hiker, camper, sailor, or mountain climber can venture very far from his or her home base without knowing what the symbols on maps stand for. Furthermore, if someone gets lost while engaged in one of these activities, it's much easier to get found by other people if he or she can give an exact location such as 33°18′ N, 125°29′ E, rather than a vague approximation like "two hours from the road that intersects the other main highway."

For people who like to use the Internet to meet people from around the world, understanding maps is a way to heighten the interest and significance of these encounters. If you're chatting with someone from a small city in Georgia, and he or she starts explaining the structure of the language, the unusual architecture of some of the buildings, or the national anthem, you'll want to be able to consult a map to see that Georgia is a small country near Russia, as well as a state in the southeastern United States.

✔ Fact Checker

To check that your child knows or can find the basic facts in this chapter, here is a fill-in activity that uses key terms defined in the preceding pages. Your child may find the answers in the list that follows the activity or may try to do the items without looking at the list. Note: Two items in the list do not fit in any blanks.

SENTENCE-COMPLETION CHALLENGE

1. Parallel, imaginary lines that run around the globe from east to west are called lines of _____.

2. Imaginary lines that run around the globe from pole to pole are called lines of _____.

3. Half of a globe (or Earth) is called a/an _____.

4. The imaginary line at 0° latitude is called the _____.

5. A mapmaker uses a _____ to represent Earth on a flat surface.

6. The part of a map that tells what the colors or other symbols stand for is called the _____.

7. The part of a map that tells how much a distance on the map is equal to in the real world is called the _____.

8. To figure out directions on a map, you can use its directional marker or _____.

compass rose	latitude	meridian	relative location
equator	legend	projection	scale
hemisphere	longitude		

Answers appear in the back, preceding the index.

? | *The Big Questions*

The following questions encourage your child to think critically rather than simply recall facts. If necessary, review the specific information from the preceding pages that will help your child make the appropriate inferences to come up with reasonable answers.

1. What piece of information that you didn't previously know about globes and maps did you get from this chapter?

2. If you had a choice of a birthday or holiday gift, would you rather get a globe of the world or a collection of maps showing the countries of the world? Explain.

3. If you want to see a lot of detail on a map, should you look for one where the scale is one inch equals one mile or one where the scale is one inch equals ten miles?

Answers

1. *Accept any reasonable answer.*
2. *Look for indications that your child understands the advantages and disadvantages of globes and of maps.*
3. *A map where the scale is one inch equals one mile*

🎖 | *Skills Practice*

The following activities give your child practice in applying the skills basic to social studies. For some of the activities, your child may need to review the information in the preceding pages.

A.   MAKING A MAP

Help your child with each step of this project, perhaps making a map of your own at the same time.

1. From the following list of different types of maps or from your imagination, pick one that you would like to make.

   a map of how to get to your room in your home

   a street map of your neighborhood

   a map of a nearby park

   a map of where to find a treasure that you will hide

2. Make a list of the things to include on your map—natural things such as hills and streams and people-made objects such as buildings.

3. Think of the things that you can show on your map as symbols, or pictures. Do a rough draft of a legend for your map.

4. Make a practice sketch of your map. It can be in black and white.

5. Make a final version of your map, using colors if possible.

Evaluating Your Child's Skills: In order to succeed with this task, your child needs to work slowly and thoughtfully. If your child has trouble pacing himself or herself, do not give the entire assignment at one time; break it into tasks to be distributed over several days.

B. GRAPHIC ORGANIZER FOR PLACE AND LOCATION

Raise your child's awareness of the difference between place and location by asking him or her to fill in the following chart—or one like it—based on the examples.

Place	Description of Place	Location of Place
Brandeis High School	school where my aunt used to teach English; huge—must have 3,000 kids; modern brick-and-tile building, 3 stories high	west side of Columbus Avenue between 85th and 84th Streets in Manhattan (northeast of the Planetarium Post Office)
Anchorage	city in central southern Alaska at the head of Cook Inlet; population about a quarter million (largest city in AK); famous for Iditarod Sled Dog Race	61° N latitude, 150° W longitude
My home		
Neighborhood library		
Landmark called _____ _____		

Evaluating Your Child's Skills: In order to succeed with this task, your child needs to categorize. He or she must realize that judgments (opinions) and some facts go under "Description of Place," but only hard facts go under "Location of Place." If your child has difficulty with this activity, review with him or her definitions and examples of *fact* and *opinion*.

C. PRACTICING DIRECTIONS

Your child can use the map of the United States on pages 130–131 to answer the following questions. He or she should fill in the appropriate cardinal or intermediate direction for each numbered item.

1. Oklahoma and Texas are both _____ of Kansas.
2. North Dakota is _____ of Missouri.
3. To get from Wyoming to Arkansas, you have to travel _____.
4. Utah is _____ of Nevada but _____ of Colorado.
5. In relation to Pennsylvania, Maine is _____.

Answers

1. south; 2. northwest; 3. southeast; 4. east, west; 5. northeast

☆ # Top of the Class

Following is a variety of activities children can do on their own or share in class to show that they have been seriously considering geography, including the topic of globes and maps.

REVIEWING A GEOGRAPHY WEB SITE

Send your child to the Internet to evaluate the medium, as described here.

Spend some time at www.nationalgeographic.com/kids/, and then write a review of the Web site. Consider the audience for your review to be children of your age. In the review, describe the site by telling the following:

- What categories of information it offers
- How easy or hard it is to find your way around the site
- How interactive the site is (that is, are there things the site lets you *do*?)
- Whether the site is educational, entertaining, or both
- The quality of the maps at this site
- The quality of the links that the site provides
- The cost of the site: which parts of the site are free, and which parts do you have to pay for?

At the end of your review, tell whether or not you recommend this Web site to your friends and classmates, to younger children, or to adults. You may hand the review in to your teacher.

ALTERNATE ROUTING

Before taking your child on a trip in your town or farther away, involve him or her in planning how to get there and home. The two of you will have to work with a mental map or a road map or a subway, bus, or train map. Here are questions you can ask your child. After the trip, let your child bring the map to class to share his or her experience with the teacher or classmates.

1. Where is our starting point?
2. Where do we want to go?
3. Which route would get us there quickest?
4. What alternative route could we take?
5. How do you want to return home—doing the same trip in reverse or taking another route?

CHAPTER 3
Planet Earth: Its Land, Water, and Air

NASA photo of Earth from space

This chapter focuses on planet Earth: its land, water, and air. The chapter describes our planet and offers explanations for how its land and water forms develop and change.

Word Power

The words on the following chart are underscored in the section called "What Your Child Needs to Know." Explain their meanings to your child as needed when they come up in reading or discussion. Keep the list handy for you and your child to use.

Word	*Definition*
contaminated	no longer pure or clean
elevations	distances above sea level
eruptions	explosions of lava from a volcano
inactive	no longer active (A volcano is said to be inactive when it no longer erupts.)
irrigated	provided dry land with water so that crops may be grown
molten	melted; very hot and liquid
particles	extremely small pieces
precipitation	falling moisture such as rain, snow, sleet, or hail
range	long chain of mountains
vapor	visible particles of moisture floating in the air

What Your Child Needs to Know

You may choose to use the following text in several different ways, depending on your child's strengths and preferences. You might read the passage aloud; you might read it to yourself and then paraphrase it for your child; or you might ask your child to read the material along with you or on his or her own.

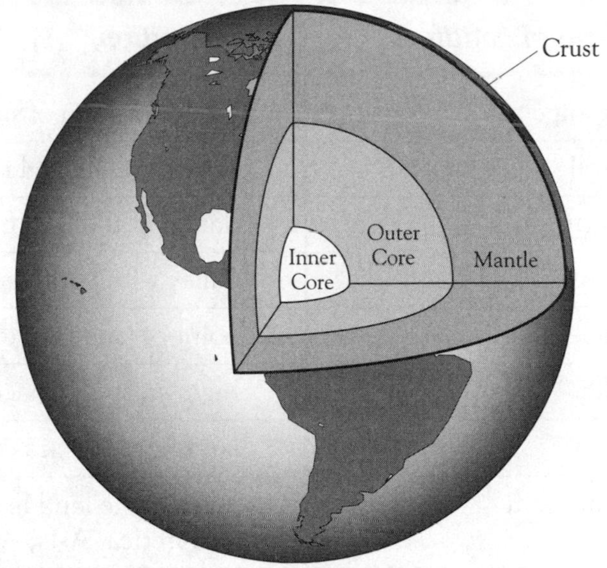

Earth's layers

INTRODUCTION TO OUR PLANET

Around 4.6 billion years ago, a swirling cloud of dust <u>particles</u> and gases came together in space. The cloud took the shape of a ball. The ball was very hot. As it cooled down, it began to develop into the planet that we now call Earth.

Earth is constantly **revolving,** or circling, around the sun in an **orbit,** or circular path. Earth takes about 365.25 days, or one year, to complete one entire orbit. While Earth is revolving, it is also **rotating,** or spinning on its **axis,** which is an imaginary line running through the North and South poles. Earth's axis is tilted, and the angle never changes. In other words, it does not tilt back and forth, but keeps the same position as the planet revolves. It takes about twenty-four hours—one entire day and night—for Earth to make one entire rotation on its axis.

EARTH'S STRUCTURE

Earth has three layers: the core, the mantle, and the crust. The **core** is Earth's center. It is very hot and is made of iron and nickel. While the inner part of the core is a solid sphere, the outer part is thought to be permanently <u>molten</u>. The **mantle,** or middle layer, is very hot and is about 1,800 miles (2,900 kilometers) thick. The outer part of the mantle consists mostly of **magma,** or melted rock, which forms a thick, hot liquid. The **crust** is the thin, solid layer of rock that covers the entire Earth, from the deepest ocean floor to the tallest mountain. It ranges in thickness from about 4 miles (6.5 kilometers) to 56 miles (89.5 kilometers). Most of the crust is covered with water or with gravel and soil. Sometimes when a giant rock appears to be jutting out of the soil, it is really an **outcropping** of the crust.

Earth's crust is not all one piece. It consists of about twenty rock slabs called **tectonic plates.** (The word *tectonic* means "structural.") Of course, all the plates are very large, but seven of them are huge, such as the one beneath the Pacific Ocean or the one that underlies most of Europe and Asia. Others are not as large. Although Earth's surface seems stationary, these plates, which "float" on Earth's liquid mantle, are constantly moving.

EARTH'S LANDFORMS

Earth's surface is characterized by many landforms, or formations. Hills, mountains, valleys, and plains are just a few. The following chart lists and defines many of the landforms found on our planet.

41

Type of Landform	Definition
archipelago	group or chain of small islands
atoll	horseshoe-shaped island formed by coral that surrounds a lagoon
butte	flat-topped hill that often has steep sides
canyon	valley with very steep sides and a flat bottom
cape	point of land that extends into a sea or an ocean
cliff	high, steep rock face
coast	land next to a sea or ocean
continent	a very large land mass (The seven continents on Earth are Africa, Antarctica, Asia, Australia, Europe, North America, and South America.)
delta	area of land shaped like a triangle where a river deposits mud, sand, or pebbles as it enters the sea or ocean
desert	dry region with fewer than 10 inches (25.4 centimeters) of rain a year
dune	hill of sand formed by blowing winds
hill	point of land that rises gently above the land surrounding it
island	body of land surrounded by water
isthmus	narrow piece of land that connects two larger pieces of land
mesa	hill or mountain with a flat top and steep sides
mountain	point of land that rises quickly to at least 1,000 feet (300 meters) above its surroundings
peninsula	piece of land surrounded by water on three sides
plain	nearly flat piece of land
plateau	flat piece of land that rises above the land around it
valley	stretch of low land that lies between hills or mountains

FORCES THAT SHAPE EARTH

The Earth we know today is nothing like the swirling cloud of dust particles and gases that formed a ball in space billions of years ago. Earth has been changing since its birth, and it is still constantly changing. Various forces continuously work upon Earth's surface to create and change its landforms. The sections that follow describe these forces and the effects they have had on some of the landforms defined in the chart.

The Movement of Tectonic Plates

Scientists are convinced that the continents—Earth's largest areas of land, now separated by water—were all joined into one **supercontinent** and that the rest of Earth was covered with one huge ocean. They call the supercontinent *Pangaea* (pan JEE uh), which means "all Earth" in Greek, and the ocean *Panthalassa,* which means "all seas." If you look at the Atlantic coastlines of South America and Africa, you can see where these continents once fitted together like pieces in a jigsaw puzzle. About 200 million years ago, the tectonic plates beneath Pangaea began to break and move apart, separating the supercontinent first into two and finally into seven continents. As the seven continents slowly moved away from each other, they reached their present locations. The continents are still slowly moving. It is likely that, in the far-distant future, they will be arranged differently on Earth's surface than they are today.

Moving tectonic plates created the seven continents, and they continue to create and change landforms. For example, as plates collide, pushing against each other, they build mountains. To understand how this happens, place a sheet of paper on a flat surface. Imagine the paper is a sheet of rock. Now imagine that tectonic plates are moving toward each other from opposite sides of the rock. Place your hands on opposite ends of the paper, and push toward the middle. The paper will begin to fold upward in the middle—like a mountain. The more you push, the higher the fold becomes. Colliding plates originally raised the great mountain range known as the Himalayas in Asia. The plates are still pushing against each other, so the Himalayas grow taller every year.

Two other ways in which the movement of tectonic plates change and shape Earth are by causing volcanoes and by causing earthquakes. A **volcano** occurs when molten rock rises to the surface and spurts up through a **vent,** or opening, in Earth's crust where two plates meet or pull apart. Melted rock known as **lava** spurts up through these vents. After thousands of eruptions, the layers of lava harden on top of each other. The Hawaiian Islands were formed by volcanic eruptions. Volcanoes also change the surface of existing land. For example, when lava pours into the ocean and hardens, coastlines grow and whole new beaches can be created. A **crater** is a bowl-shaped hollow in the mouth, or opening, of a volcano. A lake may form if the crater of an inactive volcano collapses and fills with rainwater.

An **earthquake,** which is a sudden shaking of part of Earth's surface, takes place when tectonic plates collide, pull apart, or scrape against each other as they move. Of the *millions* of earthquakes that occur each year, only a few are actually felt. But serious earthquakes can lead to lasting changes in Earth's surface. A series of quakes that hit New Madrid, Missouri, in the early 1800s raised the ground surrounding the town by about twenty feet (six meters), caused a new lake to form, and even made the Mississippi River run backward for a time! The line along which two plates have separated is called a **fault.** Movement along the San Andreas Fault in California causes about ten thousand earthquakes each year. The western plate of the San Andreas Fault is currently shifting northward. Computer projections show that in 50 million years, Los Angeles, California, may have moved as far north as Anchorage, Alaska!

Glaciers

Many changes in Earth's surface have come about as a result of **ice ages**—extremely long, cold periods when huge pieces of ice known as glaciers move slowly over land, carving and reshaping it. Scientists believe that at least four great ice ages have taken place during the past 500 million years. The most recent ice age began about 2 million years ago. During this period, the water levels of the ocean dropped about 400 feet (122 meters) below what they are now, and a **land bridge,** or strip of land, called Beringia emerged between northeastern Asia and present-day Alaska in North America. This most recent ice age was still in progress some nine or ten thousand years ago, when people are believed to have walked over the land bridge in a migration from Asia to Alaska. Once the ice melted, the water levels rose again and covered the land bridge. Today, Alaska is separated from Asia by a body of water called the Bering Sea. Yet, some scientists believe that the ice age that created and then covered the land bridge has not yet ended.

This is how a glacier forms. In a high place where it is very cold, so much snow falls that it never completely melts. Under the weight of all the snow that piles up, the snow underneath turns into a sheet of ice and is forced to move, like a river of ice, down the side of a mountain, through valleys, and over flat land, until it reaches the ocean. There the ice breaks apart and forms **icebergs.** Moving glaciers cut sharp cliffs into mountainsides, carve out valleys, create lakes, and plow down forests. They have also built up mountains, such as the Matterhorn in the Swiss Alps. Sometimes glaciers smooth out the land, but other times they dig deep holes into it. Of course, the movement of glaciers is extremely slow.

Weathering and Erosion

When wind, rain, and snow break rocks down into gravel, sand, or soil, this is called weathering. In the Namib Desert in Africa, weathering has left some rocks with large, irregular holes in them. When wind, water, or ice wear away the surface of the land, this is called erosion. Moving water causes most erosion. What starts out as a small stream can wear away the rock beneath it, creating deep canyons. The Grand Canyon in the southwestern United States formed as the Colorado River cut through the layers of rock there. Over millions of years, the river carved out the spectacular canyon that we know today. Waves carrying weathered materials have whittled large rocks into arches and columns, like those seen in Canada's Bay of Fundy. Arches form as waves, sand, and pebbles pound against both sides of a rock wall that extends into the water. The center of the rock gives way, leaving an arch. When the top part of the arch collapses, the rock columns on the sides remain.

Wind also sculpts Earth's surface into dramatic shapes. Wind carries small particles such as dust, sand, and ash from volcanoes. These particles have worn away the sides of cliffs much the way sandpaper changes the shape of a piece of wood.

Weathering and erosion build up land as well. Moving water carries weathered materials, such as gravel, sand, and rocks, to the ocean, where they are deposited on the ocean floor. Although it may take thousands of years, these materials eventually may build up into new land. Small particles carried by the wind over land have formed the large fields of sand dunes that can be found in the Middle East and in parts of Africa.

Human Activity

Earth's surface has also undergone substantial changes as a result of human activity (see Chapter 5). Humans have cut down forests, rerouted or stopped the flow of rivers, filled in wetlands, and leveled mountains. Recent studies have shown that close to half of Earth's surface is now different from how it would be in its natural state without human activity. Some of these effects are positive. For example, land that was once too dry to farm has been irrigated so that people can grow crops on it. But many of the effects of this human activity are negative and lasting. For example, when forests are cut down, the exposed soil becomes less anchored and less able to hold water. When it rains, often the water will no longer soak into the soil. In Bangladesh, where whole forests have been cut down at the foot of mountains, floods have become more common than when the forests stood. Present human activity, such as the release of carbon dioxide from cars, trucks, and factories, is very likely to effect Earth in the future. According to many scientists, carbon dioxide and other gases surrounding the planet have led to **global warming** over the past century. Temperatures around the world have risen slightly since the 1870s. The United Nations' Intergovernmental Panel on Climate Change has issued warnings that by 2100, Earth's temperature could increase by several degrees Celsius, which would cause glaciers to melt and ocean levels to rise by almost three feet (approximately one meter). Such a rise in the ocean level could mean that substantial areas of land in countries around the world would be covered by water.

EARTH'S WATER

The total amount of water on Earth never changes. In a process known as the **water cycle,** Earth's water moves from the oceans, to the air, and then back again to the oceans. As heat warms the water in rivers, lakes, and oceans, it **evaporates** and changes from liquid to gas. This gas, which is in the form of vapor, rises into the atmosphere, where it cools down. The water vapor **condenses** in the air and turns back into liquid to form clouds, fog, or ice. These droplets then fall back to Earth as rain, snow, sleet, hail, or drizzle. They soak into the ground and collect in lakes and streams, and eventually drain back to the ocean. Then the process begins again.

Only about 3 percent of the planet's water is freshwater—the other 97 percent is saltwater. Most of Earth's freshwater is frozen in glaciers and ice

Water cycle

sheets. However, rivers, lakes, and **groundwater**—water found beneath Earth's surface—are the main sources of freshwater for humans.

Oceans and Seas

The oceans, which cover about 70 percent of Earth's surface, are the bodies of water that separate the continents. They are the largest bodies of water on Earth. The oceans are never still, because they are kept in constant motion by the wind, which causes waves and **currents**—"rivers" of water that are warmer or colder than the surrounding water. Ocean water is salty.

If you explored the bottom of the ocean, you would find many formations similar to those found on land. For example, the ocean floor has its own deep canyons, steep cliffs, wide plains, and erupting volcanoes. In fact, the Mid-Oceanic Ridge is the longest mountain range on Earth, but most of it is hidden beneath the ocean. It circles Earth for more than forty thousand miles (sixty-four thousand kilometers) under the water, and at some places, it is more than one thousand miles (sixteen hundred kilometers) wide. Some mountains in this range break above the surface of the water. Easter Island, in the South Pacific, and Iceland, a country in the North Atlantic Ocean, are really the tops of underwater mountains.

A **sea** is usually defined as a body of water that is partly surrounded by land. A sea is actually an "arm" of the ocean, and so it also contains saltwater.

Rivers and Lakes

Rivers and lakes are the most important sources of usable freshwater. A river is a large, natural stream of water that flows to a larger body of water such as a lake or the ocean. The beginning of the river is called the **source,** and the end of a river is called the **mouth.** A river's source may be melting ice from a glacier or a mountain, an overflowing lake, or a spring of water coming out of the ground. A smaller stream that flows into a river is called a **tributary** of the river. A river and its tributaries make up a **river system.** A river system drains the land through which it runs of groundwater and water from <u>precipitation</u>. The area that is drained is called a **watershed.** The largest river system in the world—that of the Amazon River in South America—carries about 20 percent of Earth's water to the Atlantic Ocean.

A lake is a body of water, usually fresh, that is completely surrounded by land. Lakes form in four different ways: a crater left by a volcano fills with water; ice from a glacier carves out a depression, or low area, which fills with water as the ice melts; a shift in tectonic plates creates a depression that fills with water; people create artificial lakes by digging a depression and filling it with water or by damming up a river. The water in lakes may come from melting ice, rivers, groundwater, or natural underground springs.

There is some confusion regarding the terms *lake* and *sea.* The Caspian Sea, located between Europe and Asia, is salty, but it is actually considered a lake because it is entirely enclosed by land. Another lake that contains salt is Great Salt Lake in Utah.

Lakes vary greatly in size. While some lakes are so shallow that you can wade across them, the world's deepest lake, Lake Baikal in Russia, reaches 1 mile (1.6 kilometers) below the water's surface. The world's largest lake is the Caspian Sea, with an area of 143,240 square miles (371,000 square kilometers).

Bodies of Water Defined

The following chart lists and defines some of the many types of bodies of water found on Earth.

Body of Water	Definition
bay	curved area along an ocean coastline or a seashore where the water juts into the land; smaller than a gulf
canal	human-made waterway created to carry water from one place to another or to be used by ships; locks—large chambers formed by placing two gates across the canal—may help ships pass within the canal
gulf	large area of sea or ocean that is partly surrounded by land
harbor	body of water sheltered by natural or human-made barriers
lagoon	shallow body of calm water separated from the sea by a narrow strip of land
lake	body of water, usually fresh, that is completely surrounded by land

Body of Water	Definition
reservoir	natural or human-made lake where water is collected and stored for use
river	large, natural stream of water that flows to a larger body of water such as a lake or the ocean
sea	body of water that is an "arm" of the ocean, partly surrounded by land
sound	a wide waterway that links two large bodies of water or separates an island from the main body of a continent
strait	narrow body of water that connects two larger bodies of water
stream	a body of flowing water that runs from higher to lower ground; usually a smaller body of water than a river
waterfall	steep fall of water from a river or stream

AIR

Surrounding Earth is a layer of gases that is about one thousand miles (sixteen hundred kilometers) thick. This layer is called the **atmosphere.** The gases in the atmosphere—notably oxygen and carbon dioxide (CO_2)—are essential to life on Earth. Animals need oxygen to live, and plants need CO_2. While the atmosphere holds in heat from the sun, it also screens out the sun's dangerous rays. Without the atmosphere, we would freeze at night and be scorched by the sun during the day.

Scientists divide the atmosphere into five layers. Starting from the layer closest to Earth, they are the troposphere, the stratosphere, the mesosphere, the exosphere, and the thermosphere. The **troposphere,** where clouds and weather form, contains most of the gases and water vapor in Earth's atmosphere. It also contains dust particles. The **stratosphere** contains 19 percent of the atmosphere's gases. It also contains the **ozone layer,** a layer of pale blue gas called **ozone** that absorbs harmful rays from the sun. In the **mesosphere,** temperatures reach below −100° F (−38° C). Temperatures here get colder with height. The narrow **exosphere** is considered the border between Earth and what we call space. This is the region of the atmosphere where satellites revolve around Earth. The atmosphere's highest layer, the **thermosphere,** reaches about 400 miles (644 kilometers) above Earth's surface. Temperatures in this layer get warmer with height.

Unfortunately, Earth's atmosphere has become increasingly <u>contaminated</u> over the past several hundred years. Air pollution can pose serious health risks to humans, animals, and plants. One form of air pollution is known as **acid rain.** Pollutants in the air, such as the gases released by burning gasoline, oil, and coal, combine with sunlight and moisture to form acid. These acids fall to Earth with rain. The acid rain can kill off entire forests, pollute water, and damage buildings. Another common type of air pollution is **smog,** which is air that is highly contaminated from automobile emissions and factory smoke. Smog affects the environment by causing damage to animals, plants, and forests (see Chapter 5). Emissions containing carbon dioxide and other gases create what is known as the **greenhouse effect** by trapping heat from the sun and causing global warming. Other gases used in cleaning fluids, in some plastics, in spray cans, and to help keep refrigerators cold are causing damage to the ozone layer, increasingly exposing us to the sun's harmful rays. These gases are called **chlorofluorocarbons** (KLAW roh FLAW roh CAR buns), or **CFCs.**

Weather and Climate

Weather is the day-to-day, even the hour-to-hour, change in atmosphere. The most important influences on weather are temperature, precipitation in the atmosphere, and wind.

Climate is the usual or average weather in a specific area over a long period of time. Climate refers both to the temperature and to the amount of precipitation in the atmosphere. Following are the four main factors that determine a region's climate:

1. *Distance from the equator.* Because Earth's axis is tilted, the sun's rays hit the tropics directly, but they hit the part of Earth around the poles at a sharp angle. As you go from the equator to the poles, the sun's rays become less direct and more slanted. This explains why tropical climates are warmer than climates in higher latitudes—that is, farther away from the equator.

2. *Elevation.* At higher elevations, such as in mountain ranges, the temperature is cooler because the air there is thinner and does not hold as much of the sun's heat. For example, Cayambe, in South America's Andes Mountains, sits directly on the equator, but the top of its peak is covered with snow year-round.

3. *Movement of air and water.* Warm air and water are carried by wind and ocean currents from the tropics toward the poles. Cold air and water travel away from the North and South poles toward the tropics. Thus, a wind coming from the north carries cold air and causes colder temperatures, while a wind coming from the south carries warm air and causes warmer temperatures.

4. *Nearness to large bodies of water.* Coastal regions have a more moderate climate than regions that are in the middle of a continent; that is, they are warmer in winter and cooler in summer. This is because water temperatures do not change as much or as fast as air temperatures do. Air moving over the ocean is cooled in summer and warmed in winter.

These four factors all work together to create a region's climate. Let's look at two examples:

- A current called the Gulf Stream brings warm water from the Gulf of Mexico all the way across the Atlantic Ocean to the area around the British Isles. For this reason, the British Isles are warmer than other parts of the main European continent are at a similar distance north of the equator.
- San Francisco, California, located on the Pacific Ocean, rarely sees temperatures above 70° F (21° C). In Modesto, California, which is 100 miles (160 kilometers) directly east of San Francisco (farther from the ocean), summer temperatures typically hover around 90° F (32° C).

Climatologists, scientists who study the climate, divide the world into climate zones (see Chapter 4). While there are several different ways of doing so, one widely used system divides climates into twelve main categories. The following chart introduces Earth's different climates and indicates at which latitudes they occur.

CLIMATES OF THE WORLD

Latitudes	Climate Type	Brief Description	Example
Tropical (near equator)	Tropical wet	The climate is mostly warm and wet, with little seasonal change.	Tropical rain forest such as lands around the Amazon River in South America
	Tropical wet and dry (tropical savanna)	Most of the year's rain falls during the wet season. The rest of the year is hot and dry.	Southern India, where the wet season is called the **monsoon**
Middle latitudes	Marine west coast	Winters are rainy and mild; summers are cool.	Northern California; British Isles
	Mediterranean	Winters are rainy and mild; summers are hot and dry.	Italy; Spain; southern California; southern Australia
	Humid continental	Winters are long, cold, and snowy. Summers are short and may be quite hot.	Northern central portion of United States
	Humid subtropical	Rain is heaviest during hot summers. Winters are short and mild.	Southeastern United States
High latitudes	Subarctic	Winters are very cold. Temperatures rise above freezing during the summers.	Northern Russia, most of Alaska
	Tundra	Always cold, but the top few inches of ground thaw during the summer. There are no trees, but grasses and wildflowers grow in the tundra.	Northernmost areas of Canada, coastal areas of Greenland
	Ice cap	Climate is always bitterly cold. No vegetation grows here, but some funguslike plants called **lichens** grow on rocks.	Antarctica; most of Greenland
All latitudes	Desert	Less than 10 inches (25 centimeters) of rain falls in a year. Only plants such as cactuses can survive.	Sahara Desert in Africa; central Australia
	Semiarid (steppes)	Rainfall averages 10 to 20 inches (25 to 51 centimeters) per year. Bushes and short grasses cover the landscape. Semiarid climates usually surround deserts.	Atacama Desert in Chile; Denver, Colorado; area just south of Sahara Desert in Africa
	High elevations	Temperatures are cool or cold all year. Higher in the mountains, the temperature drops. Above the **timberline,** no trees grow. Even in the tropics, peaks of the highest mountains are covered with snow.	Mt. Kilimanjaro in Africa, high peaks of the Andes Mountains in Peru

EARTH AND THE SUN

The sun plays an all-important role in Earth's survival as a planet that can support life. Therefore, we can't offer a description of Earth without considering the effects of the planet's movement in space around the sun. It is this movement, described at the beginning of this chapter, that causes day and night and seasonal changes.

Day and Night

One complete rotation of Earth on its axis takes about twenty-four hours. The part of Earth lit by the sun during a twenty-four-hour rotation has daylight, while the part the sun does not reach has darkness, or night. That means that while it is afternoon in San Francisco, California, it is night on the other side of the globe in London, England. Because different parts of Earth experience day and night at different times, people have divided the world into **time zones.** The following chart provides facts about how time zones work.

FACTS ABOUT TIME ZONES AROUND EARTH

Features of Time Zones

There are twenty-four time zones.

Each is the width of around 15 degrees of longitude, but is adjusted to follow international boundaries or to avoid separating cities and towns from neighbors by a time difference.

They are generally one hour apart.

There are a few half-hour and quarter-hour time zones.

Features of the International Date Line

It is located at 180 degrees longitude.

It marks the beginning of each new calendar day.

Places east of the line are one calendar day behind places west of it. For example, if you leave Sydney, Australia, on a Monday and fly to Buenos Aires, Argentina, you will be flying into Sunday.

Times zones make it more convenient for people to talk about the time of day. If we did not divide the world into time zones, people in some places would be going to sleep at two o'clock in the afternoon or even eight o'clock in the morning.

Seasons

The word *season* really has two meanings. When we talk about **seasons,** we are usually referring to what the weather is like at different times of year. In the northeastern United States, there are four seasons. In summer, it is hot; in the fall, the weather grows cooler and the leaves fall from the trees; in winter, it is cold and may snow; in the spring, the weather gets warmer and leaves and flowers begin to grow again. But in places where the climate is tropical wet and dry, there are only two seasons: the dry season and the rainy season.

Although climatic seasons differ in different parts of the world, **astronomical seasons** are determined by the position of Earth in relation to the sun at different times of year. Because Earth's axis is tilted, at the point in the planet's revolution that occurs around June 21, the North Pole leans toward the sun and the South Pole leans away. At this time, summer begins in the Northern Hemisphere, and winter begins in the Southern Hemisphere. Because the tilt of Earth's axis never changes, half a year later, around December 21 when Earth is on the other side of the sun, the South Pole leans toward the sun and the North Pole leans away. Winter begins in the Northern Hemisphere, and summer begins in the Southern Hemisphere.

Another way to explain the astronomical seasons is to note that each year, around June 21, the sun appears directly overhead at the tropic of Cancer—the tropic north of the equator. Six months later, about December 21 when Earth is on the opposite side of the sun, the sun appears directly overhead at the tropic of Capricorn—the tropic south of the equator. These dates are called the **solstices.** The June solstice marks the beginning of summer in the Northern Hemisphere. On this day, the period of daylight is the longest it will be all year and the period of darkness the shortest. In the Southern Hemisphere, winter begins on this day. The December solstice marks the beginning of summer in the Southern Hemi-

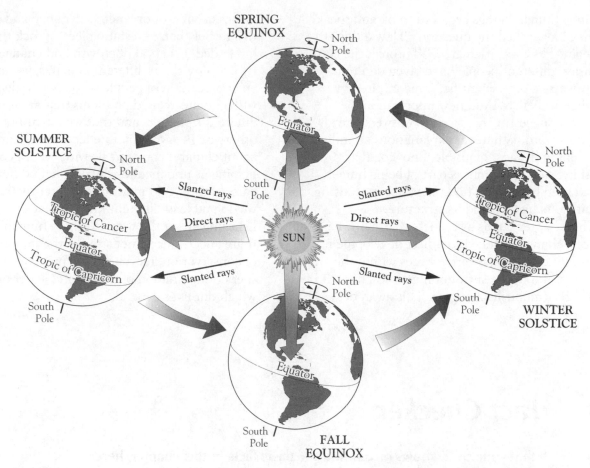

Seasons

sphere and the beginning of winter in the Northern Hemisphere, where the period of darkness is the longest it will be all year. The **equinox** is a period when the sun appears directly overhead at the equator. The equinoxes occur about March 21 and September 23. During the equinoxes, all over the world, there is the least difference between number of hours of daylight and darkness. The equinoxes signal the beginning of spring and fall, depending on whether you are in the Northern or the Southern Hemisphere.

In the tropics, the periods of light and darkness never differ greatly in length, because the sun's rays are always fairly direct. At the poles, periods of light and darkness differ greatly in length with the changing seasons. All winter, there is practically no period of sunlight at all, and all summer, there is practically no darkness.

! *Implications*

To answer the question, "Why does all this matter?" or "What does it mean?," share the following insights with your child.

• Few residents of Earth are untouched by the beauty of our planet's varied landscapes—a soaring mountain range, a still lake mirroring the colors of autumn trees, towering rock formations in the desert, ocean waves pounding against a rocky coast. Knowing something about how these wonders of nature came to be adds depth and meaning to our appreciation of our Earth's beauty.

- Since human beings began to think and speak, they have asked the question, "How did Earth begin? How was it created?" Through the centuries, different people have given different answers—some scientific, some inspired by religious beliefs. And new information is always suggesting revisions to answers already put forward. Whatever explanations an individual finds most plausible, knowing that asking such questions is part of being human will help him or her find relevance in studying Earth, its history, and its structure.

- This chapter builds awareness that Earth has been changing since its earliest development and that, due to powerful forces within the planet and in the surrounding atmosphere, it is still continuously changing. This awareness makes us view our planet as dynamic and active rather than as a static piece of rock that has ended its period of growth and change.

- By learning about different climates, we gain an appreciation of people who have to deal with climate-related problems that are totally different from ours and that we might not otherwise be aware of. In effect, then, learning about climates connects us with other people, helping us understand why people in different parts of the world may dress differently than we do and lead different kinds of lives.

- Learning about the ways in which human activity affects our planet stresses the importance of conservation, recycling, and preventing further contamination of the air and water on which our lives depend.

✔ *Fact Checker*

To check that your child knows or can find the basic facts in this chapter, here is a matching activity based on geographical terms defined in the chapter.

GEOGRAPHY MATCHUP

Match each term in the left-hand column with the correct definition in the right-hand column.

Terms

1. strait ____
2. sound ____
3. mesa ____
4. peninsula ____
5. gulf ____
6. plain ____
7. plateau ____
8. isthmus ____
9. canal ____
10. bay ____

Definitions

a. hill or mountain with flat top and steep sides

b. curved area along an ocean coastline or a seashore where the water juts into the land; smaller than a gulf

c. nearly flat piece of land

d. human-made waterway created to carry water from one place to another or to be used by ships

e. flat piece of land that rises above the land around it

f. a wide waterway that links two large bodies of water or separates an island from the main body of a continent

g. large area of sea or ocean that is partly surrounded by land

h. piece of land surrounded by water on three sides

i. narrow piece of land that connects two larger pieces of land

j. narrow body of water that connects two larger bodies of water

Answers appear in the back, preceding the index.

? The Big Questions

The following questions encourage your child to think critically rather than simply recall facts. If necessary, review the specific information from the preceding pages that will help your child make the appropriate inferences to come up with reasonable answers.

1. Based on the causes of air pollution discussed in this chapter, what are a few things individuals can do to try to prevent air pollution? What can the government do? What is one problem that stands in the way of government controls to reduce air pollution?
2. Volcanoes and earthquakes are usually considered terrible natural disasters that harm and even kill many people. Yet this chapter does not describe either a volcanic eruption or an earthquake as something bad. Why do you think this is?
3. People who live in different climates often have different cultures and customs. For example, cultures that have developed in desert climates differ from cultures that have developed in subarctic climates. Why do you think this is so?

How might thinking about this question help you to understand and accept differences among peoples from cultures other than your own?

Possible Answers

1. *Since much air pollution is caused by emission of carbon dioxide from cars, individuals can reduce air pollution by carpooling, by using public transportation, and by walking or biking when possible. They can also keep use of materials containing chlorofluorocarbons to a minimum. The government can pass laws requiring car manufacturers and factories to install equipment that will reduce harmful emissions. However, such equipment is expensive, and the cost is passed on to consumers who buy cars or other products made in factories. For this reason, laws controlling air pollution are seen by many as being bad for the country's economy.*
2. *This chapter considers natural forces only with respect to how they shape Earth's surface. From this perspective, volcanoes and earthquakes are neither good nor bad. Only their effects on human life can be judged in this way.*
3. *Knowing that cultures develop differently partially in response to differences in environment helps us to accept cultural diversity rather than view cultures different from our own as merely foreign or strange.*

Skills Practice

The following activities give your child practice in applying the skills basic to social studies. For some of the activities, your child may need to review the information in the preceding pages.

A. BUILDING A MODEL

One way of gaining deeper understanding of physical concepts is to build a model that translates a verbal explanation into something visual and active. Help your child gather the materials he or she will need to build this simple model volcano. The explanation following the instructions tells how the model is similar to an actual volcano.

Model Volcano

Materials: Unopened plastic bottle of soda water or seltzer, red food coloring

Instructions:

1. Look at the soda or seltzer. It looks like plain water. Then slowly unscrew the cap of the bottle. You will see bubbles, but when you screw the cap back on, they will disappear. The bubbles are a gas called carbon dioxide. When the bottle is tightly

closed, the air pressure inside keeps the carbon dioxide from dissolving, but when the bottle is open, there is less pressure inside. Then the gas forms bubbles that you can see.

2. Pour enough food coloring into the bottle so that the soda or seltzer looks red. The color makes it easier to see the bubbles.
3. Shake the bottle.
4. Unscrew the cap, holding the bottle away from your face and over a sink or basin. This will make the pressure inside the bottle drop suddenly. Bubbles will form and "erupt" from the open top.

Explanation: The magma in Earth's mantle holds dissolved gas, as does the soda or seltzer in the bottle. Tremendous pressure beneath Earth's surface keeps the gas in the magma dissolved. As the magma rises toward an opening in Earth's surface—the vent in a volcano—the pressure falls, and the gas forms bubbles. When the magma reaches the opening in the volcano, the bubbles explode upward and out. They erupt, as did the bubbles in the soda bottle. Magma pours down the sides of the volcano as the colored liquid poured down the sides of the bottle.

In Your Own Words: Now, in your own words, write an explanation for how the model volcano you made is like a real volcano.

Suggested Answer

The bottle is like a volcano because it has an opening at the top. The liquid in the bottle is like the magma in Earth's mantle because it holds dissolved gases. Both the liquid in the bottle and the magma are under pressure that keeps the gas from forming bubbles, but as the gas rises, the pressure is lowered. Bubbles form and escape, or erupt, from the opening.

Evaluating Your Child's Skills: Successful completion of this activity requires the ability to follow instructions and to comprehend the explanations given. Your child also needs to translate the explanations into his or her own words. If necessary, review with your child the material about volcanoes in this chapter.

B.   DRAWING DIAGRAMS

Make sure your child understands the difference between a picture and a diagram. A person drawing a picture of something tries to make the drawing look as much as possible like the thing itself. A diagram is meant to give information about something, not to resemble the thing realistically.

Look in this chapter at the charts that list and define types of landforms and bodies of water found on Earth. Choose two or three terms from each chart. Using the definitions on the charts to help you, draw a diagram illustrating each term you have chosen. Be sure to label your diagrams.

Answers

Accept diagrams that match the definitions given on the charts.

Evaluating Your Child's Skills: Your child does not need to have artistic ability to successfully complete this activity. He or she does need to be able to translate verbal information into visual information. If your child has trouble with this activity, use a reference book such as an atlas or an illustrated encyclopedia to find the landforms or bodies of water he or she has chosen to represent.

☆ *Top of the Class*

Children interested in delving more deeply into the topics covered in this chapter can choose one or more of the following activities. They may do the activities for their own satisfaction or report in class on what they have done to show that they have been seriously considering Earth's physical characteristics.

INTERNET SEARCH: RECENT CHANGES ON EARTH'S SURFACE

This activity requires your child to do some research on the Internet.

Most changes in Earth's surface take a very long time to come about. But some occur quite suddenly and dramatically. Search the Internet for geographical news about changes in Earth's surface that have occurred in recent history.
Here are two examples:

- The Loma Prieta earthquake, which hit northern California in 1989, split huge cracks in the ground, created sinkholes, and caused landslides that reshaped the coastline.
- Venice, Italy, has sunk about nine inches (twenty-four centimeters) in the past hundred years, and by the year 2050, it may have sunk another twenty inches (fifty centimeters).

One way to begin your search: using your favorite search engine, type in the key words *natural disasters*.

RESEARCH: THE RICHTER SCALE

Help your child to find out how the Richter scale measures the intensity and seriousness of an earthquake. Briefly, the Richter scale is a mathematical tool developed in 1935 by Charles Richter to measure how much energy an earthquake releases. Each number on the scale indicates a thirty-two-times increase over the previous number. A quake that measures 2.0 can barely be noticed, whereas a quake that measures 6.0 or more is considered major.

Use an encyclopedia, the Internet, or other reference tools to find out what the Richter scale is used for and how it works. (Hint: it has something to do with earthquakes.) Share the information you find with your class when you are discussing earthquakes.

BOOKS TO READ AND RECOMMEND IN CLASS

Suggest that your child read one of the following titles to find out more about the topics covered in this chapter.

Bramwell, Martyn. *Weather.* Franklin Watts, 1994.

Farndon, John. *How the Earth Works.* Reader's Digest Association, 1992.

Lambert, David. *The Kingfisher Young People's Book of Oceans.* Kingfisher, 1997.

Perham, Molly, and Julian Rowe. *Landscapes* (*Mapworlds* series). Watts, 1996. Defines and illustrates the world's basic landforms.

CHAPTER 4
Natural Regions of Earth: Biomes

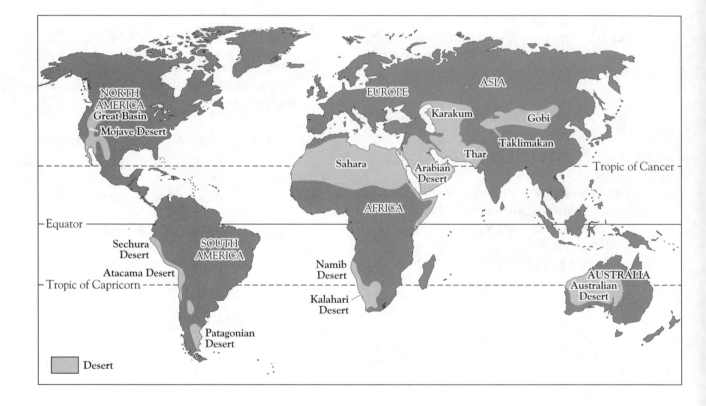

NORTH AMERICA
Great Basin
Mojave Desert

EUROPE

ASIA

Karakum

Gobi

Taklimakan

Sahara

Thar

Arabian Desert

Tropic of Cancer

AFRICA

Equator

Sechura Desert

SOUTH AMERICA

Atacama Desert

Namib Desert

AUSTRALIA
Australian Desert

Tropic of Capricorn

Kalahari Desert

Patagonian Desert

Desert

These maps show that places in different parts of the world can resemble one another. The map on the left shows parts of the world that are deserts; the map on the right shows parts of the world that are tropical rain forests. The chapter tells about deserts and rain forests in more detail and also examines five other kinds of places on the planet.

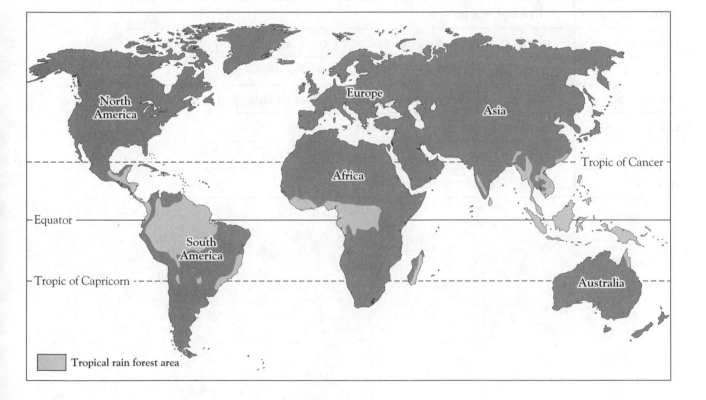

North America

Europe

Asia

Tropic of Cancer

Africa

Equator

South America

Tropic of Capricorn

Australia

Tropical rain forest area

Word Power

Word	*Definition*
adapted	suited to the conditions in which a plant or animal lives
altitude	distance above sea level
arid	dry
dormant	alive but not growing
funguses	plants with no leaves, flowers, or roots—for example, mushrooms
hibernate	spend most of the winter in a dormant, sleeplike state
microscopic	smaller than an eye can see without a tool to enlarge the object
migrate	move from one place to another
precipitation	falling moisture such as rain, snow, sleet, or hail
reflects	casts back light from a surface

What Your Child Needs to Know

You may choose to use the following text in several different ways, depending on your child's strengths and preferences. You might read the passage aloud; you might read it to yourself and then paraphrase it for your child; or you might ask your child to read the material along with you or on his or her own.

INTRODUCTION TO BIOMES

Geographers began carefully observing parts of the world twenty-five hundred years ago. As they looked at more and more places, they noticed that some parts of the world resemble one another. That is, two or more places in different parts of the world may have the same or related plants and may have animals with similar features or behaviors.

Geographers went on to classify, or group, places by the types of living things found there. They call groups of places with similar plant and animal life *biomes*. For example, there are deserts all over the world, and they all have similar plant and animal life. The scientific definition of a biome is "a natural community of organisms that takes up a large area."

After observing places all over Earth, geographers concluded that there really are only a few kinds of biomes. Depending on the ways they describe or categorize the plants and animals all over the planet, some geographers say there are seven kinds of biomes, while other geographers say there are thirteen kinds. To keep matters as simple as possible here, this book will identify seven kinds and will tell how some of the seven biomes have variations, or slight differences. Here is a preview of the seven kinds of biomes. Discussion of each follows.

THE SEVEN BIOMES

Biome	Brief Description	Example
desert	large, dry area	Sahara Desert in North Africa
forest	large area thickly covered with trees and plants	Hoh Rain Forest in Washington State
grassland	large, open area of grass	Serengeti Plain in Tanzania
polar region	large, icy region around the North or South Pole	Antarctica
mountain	very high piece of land	Mount McKinley, or Denali, in Alaska
ocean	entire body or part of the body of saltwater covering Earth's surface	Pacific Ocean
wetland	large area of ground that is covered by water	Everglades in Florida

DESERTS

When you close your eyes and picture a desert, what do you see? If you are like most people, you probably see a lot of sand, blazing sunshine, and maybe a camel or two, along with a person dressed in light, flowing clothes. That picture is accurate, but it is not complete.

To get a better picture of deserts, let's begin with a better definition. A desert is an area of land that is very dry. Geographers call a place a desert if it gets ten inches (twenty-five centimeters) or less of <u>precipitation</u> a year. In some deserts, it rains only once in fifty years; in one part of the Atacama Desert in Chile, South America, there was no rain for four hundred years! So one of the best words to describe a desert is <u>arid</u>. Some deserts are said to be *semiarid*, meaning "partly dry"; semiarid deserts get all or nearly all their rain in one season of the year and are dry the rest of the time. Deserts may have an occasional river, and deserts may have water far below ground, but most of the surfaces of deserts are dry.

While all deserts are arid or semiarid, not all are sandy. In fact, most are *not* sandy. Instead, most deserts are mountainous or are made up of stones, rocks, gravel, or other substances.

Not all deserts are always hot. Some are hot some but not all of the time, and some are never hot. For example, in a desert where it may be 130° F (54° C) during the day, it may be only 40° F (4° C) at night. Then there are deserts such as the Gobi Desert in Asia and the deserts in western North America, which are cold all winter long—day and night. The areas around the North Pole and the South Pole are sometimes considered deserts also, and those areas are never hot. The polar regions can be classified as deserts because the water they contain is locked in ice year-round.

Camels have long existed in deserts, but they are not the only animals found there. Other animals found in deserts include <u>funguses</u> and bacteria; insects such as ants, locusts, spiders, and scorpions; reptiles such as snakes, lizards, and tortoises; birds such as elf owls, roadrunners, and ostriches; and rodents and small kangaroos, as well as gazelles and cheetahs. Each of these animals is well <u>adapted</u> for survival in a desert. For example, some snakes and lizards as well as kangaroos can leap across the burning-hot ground.

Some plants that survive in deserts are cactuses, which soak up water after a storm and store the water in their trunks and branches. Other desert plants have very deep roots, which can reach water far underground. Sometimes after a rainfall in a desert, many beautiful flowers bloom for a short while. They bloom from seeds that are <u>dormant</u> until the rain comes along.

Deserts exist on all continents (see Chapter 7). Deserts make up between one-quarter and one-third of all the land areas in the world. About a billion people, or one in every five people, live in deserts. They prefer parts of the desert where natural rivers flow or where water can be brought in to make crops grow.

In some deserts, people work to stop sand from blowing off dunes and traveling to grasslands. People want grasslands to stay as they are—not become more desert.

FORESTS

Forests are beautiful. They are also important natural resources. From forests, people get wood for lumber, paper, and fuel. Other products that people need from forests include rattan, wicker, turpentine, and cork. Forests are lost forever when people cut down more trees than can grow back.

How many kinds of forests are there on Earth? According to one way of counting, we have seven kinds of forests. They take up a little less than one-third of the land on Earth, and they grow on every continent except Antarctica. Wherever you find a large area covered with trees that grow so that their leaves shade the ground, you have a forest. These areas get at least thirty inches (seventy-five centimeters) of rain a year. Some forests are called **mixed forests** because they contain plants and animals from two or more of the seven kinds of forests listed here.

Forests are made up of some or all of the following layers, from the top down: the forest **canopy,** which is the tops of the tallest trees; an **understory** of smaller trees; a layer of shrubs and woody plants; and finally the forest **floor,** covered by soft-stem plants such as ferns, mosses, and wildflowers.

Tropical Forests

Some people refer to tropical forests as **jungles.**

Tropical rain forests grow in lowlands near the

equator, where the year-round wet, warm weather produces thick evergreens, such as the coconut palm. These forests are dense and heavily populated: they are home to about half of all the kinds of plants and animals on the earth. Living in the canopy are monkeys, birds, bats, and reptiles. On the ground of African rain forests, you may find gorillas, forest elephants, and buffaloes; on the ground of South American rain forests, you may find anteaters, tapirs, jaguars, pumas, and ocelots.

Tropical deciduous forests grow in hot climates where it is wet part of the year and dry part of the year. *Deciduous* describes the kinds of trees that lose their leaves for part of the year.

Temperate Forests

Temperate rain forests grow where rainfall itself may be lower than in the tropics but the air is full of ocean moisture—as in the Pacific Northwest. The trees include evergreens such as hemlock, cedar, spruce, fir, and redwood.

Temperate deciduous forests dominate where there are warm summers and cold winters. The trees in these forests have leaves that change color with the seasons and then fall off. Examples are maple trees, beeches, ash, oaks, and elms. Flying and climbing through these forests are birds, bats, squirrels, raccoons, bears, and deer.

Temperate evergreen forests grow along coasts, such as the gulf coast of the United States, where the climate is warmish. As the name suggests, these forests keep their leaves all year. Examples of the plant life include live oak, magnolia, some palms, and bromeliads.

Other Forests

Boreal forests, also called **taiga,** grow where winters are extremely cold and the short summers are cool. Spruce and fir trees grow here. These trees are called **conifers** because they produce cones. In boreal forests, you can find rabbits, wolves, deer, and moose as well as animals that either hibernate or migrate to warmer areas in the winter.

There is one more kind of forest. It grows where there are hot, dry summers, and moist, cool winters—around the Mediterranean Sea as well as in Australia, parts of South Africa, Chile, and California, and this forest has different names in each place. In California, it is known as **chaparral.** This kind of forest has lots of evergreen bushes, known as **shrubs** or **scrub.**

GRASSLANDS

Grasslands develop where there is not enough rain for many trees to grow but too much rain for a desert to form. Grasslands get between ten and thirty inches (between twenty-five and seventy-five centimeters) of rain each year.

TROPICAL GRASSLANDS

Tropical grasslands, which are also called **savannas,** grow inland at or near the equator. These regions are hot year-round, with short, rainy seasons and long, dry seasons. The Serengeti Plain in East Africa is a savanna. There, among tall grasses and scrubby trees (such as baobabs and acacias), you can find herds of animals that graze on the grasses—antelopes, wildebeests, zebras, giraffes, gazelles, rhinos, buffaloes, and elephants. Animals that hunt these grazers are cheetahs, leopards, and lions.

TEMPERATE GRASSLANDS

Temperate grasslands can exist where there are warm summers and cold winters. In North America, these grasslands are also known as **prairie,** and in other parts of the world, they are called **steppe, veld,** or **pampas.** In these places, grasses measure between 20 inches and 5 feet (half a meter and 1.5 meters). In North America, originally, wild animals such as bison grazed on the prairies, but then people introduced cows, sheep, horses, and goats. People also removed the grass and planted grains. Eventually, the wild animals disappeared.

All grasslands are also home to a huge population of insects. The insects attract birds, but in grasslands, where there are so few trees, birds build their nests on or in the ground.

POLAR REGIONS

The ice-covered regions around the North Pole and the South Pole are similar to each other but also different from each other. They are both extremely cold because they get only indirect, or slanted, sunlight, and they get it only half the year. They are cold for another reason too: the ice <u>reflects</u> rather than absorbs the sun's rays.

The biome around the North Pole is called the **Arctic.** It is made up of mostly ice-covered ocean surrounded by land areas. The biome around the South Pole is called the **Antarctic,** and it can get colder than the North Pole. It consists of the world's fifth-largest continent—ice-covered Antarctica, surrounded by ocean.

Several populated countries exist in the Arctic, but only scientists and other researchers live in the Antarctic. The Arctic region has not only dolphins, porpoises, whales, and seals but also land animals such as polar bears (that can spend long periods in the icy water, too), caribou, reindeer, foxes, hares, lemmings, and wolves—and birds such as snowy owls. The Antarctic region has no land animals except insects. In the ocean and on the fringes of the continent live four kinds of seals and five kinds of penguins, as well as fish and other birds. The Antarctic, like the Arctic, does not have as many whales as it once had. Plant life in these biomes is extremely rare.

As everywhere else, the animals in these regions are well adapted to their surroundings. For example, the bodies of dolphins, porpoises, whales, and seals all have oily fat called blubber to help these animals deal with the cold.

South of the Arctic Ocean is an area known as **tundra.** Here, a shallow layer of soil can support some plants, but they must have very short roots because just below the soil is a dense layer of **permafrost,** frozen at all times.

MOUNTAINS

A mountain is a landform that is at least one thousand feet (three hundred meters) above its surrounding area. As the boxed information shows, a mountain and a mountain range can be gigantic.

Just as you will travel through different biomes as you move from the equator toward the North or South Pole, so you can experience different biomes by moving from the base of some mountains to their peaks. Another way of saying this is to point out that changes in <u>altitude</u> can mean changes in temperature and in plant and animal life. For example, if you were to climb from the base of Mount Kilimanjaro in Africa, you would move from a tropical forest to a deciduous forest to an evergreen forest to a tundra zone. Along the way, you would go through transition zones, where one kind of forest begins to become another kind of forest. Depending on when you read this book, there may still be a zone of snow and ice at the very top of Kilimanjaro, or it will have melted because of changes in climate.

As in other biomes, the plants and animals that have survived on mountains to today have become adapted to particular conditions. For example, at certain altitudes on a mountain, small plants have fuzz to hold the heat and very long roots to keep themselves on the slope in spite of strong winds. Other examples of adaptation to mountains are the protective coat of the mountain goat and the amazing lungs of the eagle, which can breathe easily at different altitudes as it soars up and down the mountain looking for food and shelter.

If people use a mountain too much—for farming, mining, logging, and recreation—the original plant life may disappear. Without these plants holding the soil in place, landslides may occur, destroying communities in mountain valleys.

Facts about Mountains and Mountain Ranges

Every continent, as well as the seafloor, has mountains.

Tallest mountain: Mount Everest in the Himalayas—29,028 feet (8,848 meters)

Largest (in volume): Mauna Loa in Hawaii

Longest in ocean: Mid-Ocean Ridge circling Earth—40,000 miles (64,000 kilometers)

Longest on land: Andes in South America—4,000 miles (6,437 kilometers)

OCEANS AND SEAS

Saltwater now covers about three-fourths of Earth. The water exists as one continuous body flowing around the continents, but people have given names to different parts of it. From the largest to the smallest part, we have the Pacific Ocean, the Atlantic Ocean, the Indian Ocean, and the Arctic Ocean. (Some people use the name Antarctic Ocean to refer to the southern regions of the Atlantic, Pacific, and Indian oceans.) Forms of life in the ocean range in size from <u>microscopic</u> plants and animals to the blue whale, which grows to ninety feet (thirty meters).

In places, oceans are as deep as 35,800 feet (10,900 meters). Sunlight penetrates the surface of oceans and down to about 650 feet (200 meters). In this top part of the water float the microscopic plants and animals called **plankton.** The tiny animals graze on the tiny plants, and they, in turn, become food for larger animals—fish, shellfish, and even the blue whale. As oceans get deeper, darker, and colder, some animals either eat plants and other animals that drift down or go to the surface to feed. At the deepest, near-freezing depths of the ocean, some animals have organs that produce light, but the others, such as the giant squid, live in total darkness.

A sea is a part of an ocean—a part enclosed by land. Examples include the Mediterranean, Black, Red, North, and Baltic seas.

Hundreds of years ago, explorers proved that Earth is not flat, but it took until the 1920s for people to learn that the floor of the oceans is not flat, either. Instead, besides plains, which are flat, the ocean floor has mountains, canyons, and ditches (called **trenches**). The other lesson people learned is that fishing too much and polluting the oceans too much will cause serious problems for this biome and, ultimately, for themselves.

WETLANDS

Wet grounds that are always or sometimes covered by water go by many names, but the three main kinds are **swamps, marshes,** and **bogs.** Trees such as cypresses and mangroves dominate swamps, which also are home to fish, shellfish, birds, reptiles, and amphibians (animals that can live in water or on land). Marshes produce grasses rather than trees.

They also have birds, fish, shellfish, amphibians, and other animals, such as the deer of the Florida Everglades. Bogs are more common in cooler climates. Tangled vegetation in bogs chokes the water. As a result, a spongy mat called **peat** forms, and often a person can stand on the mat of a bog without getting soaking wet.

Fascinating adaptations account for some of the living things found in wetlands. For example, some plants in wetlands catch and eat insects in order to get the minerals they need. Crocodiles can live in swamps because they breathe air and so are not bothered by the lack of oxygen in most wetland waters.

People used to drain wetlands for two reasons: (1) to make more land available to build on and (2) to kill disease-carrying insects. Then people learned that animals that migrate from one biome to another need the wetlands to rest in. People also learned that they themselves need wetlands in order to prevent flooding of other land. So today people are trying to save or bring back wetlands.

☐! *Implications*

To answer the question, "Why does all this matter?" or "What does it mean?," share the following insights with your child.

- It is hard to establish clear borders between biomes, which are defined by the plants and animals that live in them. In fact, geographers do not always agree on exactly how many biomes there are in the world or how they should be classified.
- Sometimes one biome does not just end and another biome immediately begin. Between a forest biome and a grassland biome, for example, there may be a transition zone, or area.
- Some plants and biomes can exist in more than one biome. For example, wolves live in some forests as well as in the Arctic.
- Some plants and animals exist in only one biome. For example, the only place (other than a zoo) you find penguins is the Antarctic.
- Over an extremely long time, only the plants and animals that became adapted to their

surroundings managed to survive in a particular biome. For example, polar bears survived in their biome because their thick white fur, which keeps them warm, also helps them blend in with their snowy surroundings and so allows them to hunt unseen by their prey.

- All biomes face threats. Wetlands, for example, may be polluted. Grasslands can be lost because of farming. People need to work to save biomes.

 **Fact Checker**

To check that your child knows or can find the basic facts in this chapter, here is a game based on the names and descriptions of the biomes.

BIOME MATCHING GAME

For each item on the left, find a true statement about it on the right. Write the correct letter on the blank after each item. Use all descriptions, but do not use any description for more than one answer.

Biome

1. wetland ____
2. ocean ____
3. mountain ____
4. polar region ____
5. grassland ____
6. forest ____
7. desert ____

Description

a. *Arid* is a fitting word to describe this biome.

b. Zebras live in this biome.

c. This place may be home to several biomes at once.

d. Every continent but Antarctica has this biome.

e. Marshes, swamps, and bogs are examples of this biome.

f. Blubber helps animals in this biome.

g. Some animals in this biome live in permanent darkness.

Answers appear in the back, preceding the index.

? The Big Questions

The following questions encourage your child to think critically rather than simply recall facts. If necessary, review the specific information from the preceding pages that will help your child make the appropriate inferences to come up with reasonable answers.

1. Imagine that you are in a tropical rain forest in South America and that you start traveling north, heading into and through North America. What are you more likely to come across first as you move north—a forest with trees that lose leaves during some seasons or a forest with trees that produce cones? Explain your answer.

2. Generally, New York City is cold in the winter but not as cold as the polar regions. The rest of the year, New York City is not at all cold. What might a zoo in New York City do so that it can become a home to polar bears?

3. What is an advantage of living on a planet with a number of biomes? Would you prefer to live on a planet with only one biome? Why or why not?

Suggested Answers

1. *You would come across a forest with leaves that change color and fall off before you would come across a forest with cones. The second kind of forest (with cones) exists in a colder region than the first kind of forest (with leaves that change color), so the second kind of forest must be farther north, where it is colder.*

2. *To house polar bears, a zoo in New York City would need systems to keep bathing and drinking water ice cold and to keep the air very chilly also. The zoo would also have to provide food that the bears are used to.*

3. *Answers will vary but should show that your child understands that a one-biome world would probably have only a limited number of kinds of plants and animals compared with a world of many biomes.*

Skills Practice

The following activities give your child practice in applying the skills basic to social studies. For some of the activities, your child may need to review the information in the preceding pages.

A.   MAKING A GRAPHIC ORGANIZER

Many schools encourage children to use graphics to help them absorb, organize, and master new information. Teachers often use the term *graphic organizer* as a general label for a variety of charts, tables, and diagrams. Ask your child to fill in the following chart with facts about the biomes.

BIOME FACTS

	Notable Plant	Notable Animal
1. desert		
2. tropical rain forest		
3. wetland		

Answers

Other answers are possible.

1. desert: cactus; camel
2. tropical rain forest: coconut palm; gorilla
3. wetland: cypress; crocodile

Evaluating Your Child's Skills: In order to complete this activity successfully, your child will need to review the preceding pages and search for appropriate facts for each box on the chart. If he or she has trouble, simplify the task by showing the child only one column or one row at a time.

B.   CONNECTING GEOGRAPHY AND LITERATURE

Give your child a chance to see that reading a novel and learning about geography can go together. Your child may have read one or more of the following novels in class or independently. If not, now is a chance for you to read one of them together. (All the titles are still in print and are also usually available in public libraries.) Following the list of novels, you will find questions to ask your child.

Novels

Baylor, Byrd. *Hawk, I'm Your Brother.* Scribner, 1976. A story of human-animal interaction in the mountains.

George, Jean Craighead. *The Moon of the Alligators.* Crowell, 1969. A story that takes place in a wetlands biome.

Atwater, Richard. *Mr. Popper's Penguins.* Little, Brown, 1938. Written in the 1930s: the complications of moving a living thing out of a polar biome.

George, Jean Craighead. *My Side of the Mountain.* Dutton, 1959. A boy and a mountain in New York State.

MacLachlan, Patricia. *Sarah, Plain and Tall.* Harper & Row, 1985. How regions (Maine and the prairies) are similar and how they are different.

Gardiner, John Reynolds. *Stone Fox.* Harper, 1980. Life in the mountains of Wyoming.

Questions

1. What did you learn about a biome that you did not know before you read the book?
2. What are good reasons for living in or visiting the biome described in the book—either now or in the past? What are good reasons for *not* living in or visiting the biome?

Possible Answers

1. *Accept any reasonable answer.*
2. *Accept any reasonable answer that your child states and goes on to support with details.*

Evaluating Your Child's Skills: In order to complete this activity successfully, your child will need to recall information (Question 1) and compare and contrast information (Question 2). If he or she has trouble with the latter, help by making a graphic organizer like the one in Skills Practice A.

C.   EVALUATING ARGUMENTS

Help your child become aware of the powers of persuasion at the heart of advertisements that you come across in magazines or solicitations that you receive from environmental organizations. Such organizations not only ask the public to make donations but also invite the public to take other actions.

Have your child read the advertisement or solicitation. Then ask him or her the following questions. (If you do not have ads or solicitations at hand, consider visiting the Web site www.earthshare.org to learn about a federation of environmental organizations and to find links to individual charities.)

1. What is this organization asking us to do to help the planet?
2. What, if anything, does the organization say we will receive if we do as it asks?
3. Do you think we should support this group? Why or why not?

4. Since we cannot support every organization that wants to help wildlife of the planet, how do we choose which ones to support?
5. What questions about this organization should we ask before we decide whether to help it out?

> ***Evaluating Your Child's Skills:*** **In order to complete this activity successfully, your child will need to practice (and see you practice) making judgments about persuasive ads, mailings, or Web sites. If your child needs help answering the preceding questions, suggest creating a table on which you can list pros and cons about an organization and supporting it.**

D. NOTING CAUSE-EFFECT RELATIONSHIPS

> **Read one of the following causes to your child. Tell him or her that the cause is a true statement. (You do not have to use the terms *cause* and *effect*.) Then ask your child whether statement A or whether statement B is the result, or consequence, of the cause.**

1. CAUSE: Grasslands have very few or no trees.
   EFFECT?
   STATEMENT A: There are no birds in grasslands.
   STATEMENT B: Birds in grasslands build their nests *on* the ground or *in* the ground.
2. CAUSE: Some cactuses and other desert plants have thorns.
   EFFECT?
   STATEMENT A: The plants survive because animals such as kangaroos cannot eat the plants without hurting or killing themselves.
   STATEMENT B: Roses, which also have thorns, grow near the cactuses.
3. CAUSE: Very little sunlight reaches the floor of a tropical rain forest.
   EFFECT?
   STATEMENT A: Most of the animals in a rain forest spend all their time prowling around the floor to keep cool.
   STATEMENT B: The surface of a rain forest floor is relatively bare.

Answers
1. B; 2. A; 3. B

> ***Evaluating Your Child's Skills:*** **In order to complete this activity successfully, your child needs to recall facts or make inferences based on facts that you have shared with him or her about biomes. If your child needs help, demonstrate how you can arrive at the right answer by using what you know to determine that the other choice contains wrong information, leading you to eliminate it. For example, you know that there *are* birds in grasslands), so 1A is wrong, and 1B must be the effect that results from a lack of trees.**

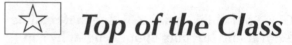 ## *Top of the Class*

> **Following is a variety of activities children can do on their own or share in class to show that they have been seriously considering the topic of biomes.**

PERSUASIVE LETTER

> **The following explanation explains the purpose of persuasive letters. Work with your child to identify an environmental issue and to write a letter persuading others to agree with you.**

People with strong opinions sometimes write letters to express themselves. They may write to a politician, or they may write a letter to the editor of a publication. On the general topic of biomes, people have opinions and write letters about everything from recycling garbage to the greenhouse effect.

Your letter should state an opinion, support the opinion with reasons, and anticipate and answer objections that a reader might raise. Share the letter—and its results—with your teacher and classmates. Was the letter published? Did you receive a response to the letter?

BRAINTEASER

Here is a puzzler to pose to your child and for him or her then to pose to classmates.

Question

From what one spot on Earth do you always travel south regardless of which way you walk?

Answer

The North Pole

TELEVISION ALERT

Here's an opportunity for actually encouraging your child to watch television.

Scan television listings to identify a program about problems or successes in a particular biome. The Discovery Channel and the National Geographic Channel and series such as *Nova* on PBS stations regularly feature such programs. Then alert your teacher and classmates to a program that sounds relevant, watch the show, and ask to hold a class discussion about its strengths and weaknesses.

WEB SITES TO EXPLORE

If your child enjoys any of the following Web sites or finds another biome-related site, he or she may want to share it with the teacher and classmates.

Biomes in General

http://library.thinkquest.org   Click "Geo-Globe" and then "Geo-Adapt" to find an interactive game.

http://mbgnet.mobot.org   Student-oriented site of the Missouri Botanical Garden.

Deserts

http://pubs.usgs.gov/gip/deserts/contents

http://www.stemnet.nf.ca/CITE/deserts.htm Includes a student project. Many of its links no longer operate, but the site is helpful in and of itself.

Oceans

http://seawifs.gsfc.nasa.gov/ocean_planet.html Smithsonian traveling exhibit.

CHAPTER 5
People and Earth

The first chapter of this book defines *geography* as "the study and explanation of Earth, its resources, and life, with particular emphasis on the description of the land, air, and water, and the distribution of plants, animals, and people." This chapter concentrates on the people and how they interact with Earth. All of us—the 6 billion living now and those who lived in the past—have had a profound impact on Earth, and Earth and the forces of nature have also affected us in many significant ways.

Word Power

The words on the following chart are underscored in the section called "What Your Child Needs to Know." Explain their meanings to your child as needed when they come up in reading or discussion. Keep this list handy for you and your child to use.

Word	Definition
census	official population count, conducted to determine total population and trends
controversy	argument
corporations	businesses
Homo sapiens	modern humans
hostilities	acts of war
industrialization	process of setting up businesses and factories
nomadic	moving from one place to another; having no fixed home
pesticides	agents for killing insects
plague	very serious disease that spreads quickly to many people and often causes death
sanitation	system for cleaning water and getting rid of waste
toleration	acceptance

What Your Child Needs to Know

You may choose to use the following text in several different ways, depending on your child's strengths and preferences. You might read the passage aloud; you might read it to yourself and then paraphrase it for your child; or you might ask your child to read the material along with you or on his or her own.

WHAT'S IN A CULTURE?

Humans are social animals, meaning most people like to live somewhere in the vicinity of other humans. Since earliest times, humans have formed **communities**—groups of people who have a common bond or interest that brings them together. Over the course of many years, the people living in a community (or in a group of communities in a region) develop an entire way of life—a culture—that is different from the practices of people living in other communities. Culture includes a group's language, religion, customs and manners, arts and crafts, government, technologies, and even attitudes toward natural surroundings.

Understanding someone's culture is made harder by the fact that a person can belong to more than one culture. For example, someone can be part of American, teenage, and tuna-fishing cultures if he or she happens to be a thirteen-year-old living in a northeastern U.S. fishing community. Furthermore, a specific culture can exist in more than one community. For example, a French-speaking culture exists in Paris, France, as well as in Montreal, Quebec, and on the Caribbean island of Martinique.

Finally, a physical community—the people in an apartment building or small-town neighborhood, for example—can contain more than one culture: unmarried singles, young families, retired people, health-club members, opera lovers, pet owners, and so on.

HOW DID CIVILIZATIONS DEVELOP?

Let's look at cultures historically. Over the course of thousands of years, some of the world's early cultures advanced and changed; they adapted to their physical surroundings as well as to events such as wars. Some cultures died out because of unfavorable surroundings, hostilities with members of a more powerful culture, or misuse of natural resources—water, air, soil, plants, animals, minerals. Cultures that managed to advance to a very high level became **civilizations.**

In addition to all the things a culture has, each civilization in history has had a complex system of government, sophisticated construction skills, written language, and division of labor into different jobs for different people. Another mark of civilizations has been concentration of lots of people in **urban,** or city, settings.

People use both the singular form and the plural form of the word *civilization*. We tend to talk about ancient *civilizations* but a single contemporary *civilization*, which we say is made up of many cultures.

The first civilizations arose about six thousand years ago, despite the fact that *Homo sapiens* had inhabited Earth for more than two hundred thousand years by that point. What took humans so long to achieve all the marks of civilization listed here? The answer is that for some reason it wasn't until about 9000 B.C. that people figured out how to grow their own food—agriculture. This was one of the most important steps toward civilization. It meant that people no longer had to move all the time to hunt and gather their food.

Once they could stay in one place, people began to develop towns and then cities. Equally important, farming helped provide more food than any one farmer needed, so not everyone had to farm. Some people could spend their time making pots or baskets. Then they could trade the pots or baskets to farmers in exchange for food.

Trade between members of a culture and then between different cultures required laws and government to make sure people followed the rules. Out of all these related events, civilizations were born; some of the earliest were in Mesopotamia, the area now known as Iraq, and in Egypt, China, and Mexico.

DEMOGRAPHY: HOW MANY PEOPLE ARE THERE?

How many people are there in the world? For that matter, how many people have lived in the world from the very beginning until today? These are questions about population, which is the total number of people in a specific area—a neighborhood, town, state, country, continent, or planet.

The study of statistics about populations is called demography. (The word *demography* comes from Greek words meaning "people writing," just as *geography*, as noted in Chapter 1, means "earth writing.")

Demographers, the scientists who analyze population statistics, look at a lot of data: census results, birth and death rates, life expectancy (how long, on average, people will live), doubling time (the amount of time it takes for a population to double, given a steady growth rate), where people live, and the current ages of a population. Based on all these numbers, demographers tell us how many people there are today and estimate how many there will be in the future.

Growth Rates

The world's population has generally been growing since humans appeared on the planet, even though for brief periods, such as in the time of a plague, it seemed that more people were dying than being born. More important, the pace of growth has been greater in modern times.

It is estimated that there were about 250 million people alive at the time of Jesus Christ, and not until about 1800 were there as many as 1 billion people on Earth. Even though there were many births, death rates were also high because of diseases, poor sanitation, wars, and weather conditions that reduced crops. However, with advances in agriculture, medicine, and transportation, the world's population sextupled—multiplied by six—in the last two centuries! In fact, the planet's population grew from approximately 2.5 billion to more than 6 billion just from 1950 to the present.

WHERE DO PEOPLE LIVE?

Throughout history, population centers have developed in places with certain geographic characteristics: sufficient rainfall, good soil for farming, waterways for distributing food and for travel, mineral riches, and so on. Only about one-third of Earth is inhabited because much of our planet doesn't have those characteristics.

Cities

All through history, the world's population has been moving toward urban centers, cities. Today, demographers estimate that more than half of the world's population lives in cities.

The movement toward cities has been dramatic in the last hundred years and relates to advances in industrialization and technology, both of which are discussed later in this chapter. England became the first urban nation toward the end of the nineteenth century, when more than half of its population began living in cities; the United States achieved that status in the early 1920s. Today, there are close to three hundred cities around the world with populations of more than a million. Fifty years ago, fewer than 300 million people lived in cities in poor countries; now, close to 2 billion reside there, and demographers predict that number will double by 2025.

Alternatives to Cities

Despite the rapid growth of cities during the last century, not everyone in the United States lives in a city. There are other settings in which Americans reside: village, town, rural community, and suburb.

The 2000 U.S. census indicated that about 218 million Americans lived in **metropolitan areas,** which consist of a city and surrounding built-up population areas. Of the 218 million, about 82 million lived inside the central city of the metropolitan area, while the other 136 million lived outside the central city—for example, in **suburbs,** which are communities on the outskirts of a central city, or in small towns or villages within commuting distance to the city. Finally, about 54 million Americans lived in nonmetropolitan areas, which include villages and towns that are more isolated than ones near a city, or in **rural communities,** defined as areas of farmland or countryside.

This is not an official census form. It is for informational purposes only.

United States Census 2000

U.S. Department of Commerce • Bureau of the Census

This is the official form for all the people at this address. It is quick and easy, and your answers are protected by law. Complete the Census and help your community get what it needs — today and in the future!

Start Here

Please use a black or blue pen.

1. How many people were living or staying in this house, apartment, or mobile home on April 1, 2000?

☐ Number of people

INCLUDE in this number:
- foster children, roomers, or housemates
- people staying here on April 1, 2000 who have no other permanent place to stay
- people living here most of the time while working, even if they have another place to live

DO NOT INCLUDE in this number:
- college students living away while attending college
- people in a correctional facility, nursing home, or mental hospital on April 1, 2000
- Armed Forces personnel living somewhere else
- people who live or stay at another place most of the time

2. Is this house, apartment, or mobile home — *Mark ☒ ONE box.*
- ☐ Owned by you or someone in this household with a mortgage or loan?
- ☐ Owned by you or someone in this household free and clear (without a mortgage or loan)?
- ☐ Rented for cash rent?
- ☐ Occupied without payment of cash rent?

3. Please answer the following questions for each person living in this house, apartment, or mobile home. Start with the name of one of the people living here who owns, is buying, or rents this house, apartment, or mobile home. If there is no such person, start with any adult living or staying here. We will refer to this person as Person 1.

What is this person's name? *Print name below.*

Last Name

First Name | MI

4. What is Person 1's telephone number? *We may call this person if we don't understand an answer.*

Area Code + Number

5. What is Person 1's sex? *Mark ☒ ONE box.*
☐ Male ☐ Female

6. What is Person 1's age and what is Person 1's date of birth?

Age on April 1, 2000

Print numbers in boxes

Month | Day | Year of birth

→ **NOTE: Please answer BOTH Questions 7 and 8.**

7. Is Person 1 Spanish/Hispanic/Latino? *Mark ☒ the "No" box if not Spanish/Hispanic/Latino.*
- ☒ **No,** not Spanish/Hispanic/Latino
- ☐ Yes, Mexican, Mexican Am., Chicano
- ☐ Yes, other Spanish/Hispanic/Latino — *Print group.* ⟋
- ☐ Yes, Puerto Rican
- ☐ Yes, Cuban

8. What is Person 1's race? *Mark ☒ one or more races* to indicate what this person considers himself/herself to be.
- ☐ White
- ☐ Black, African Am., or Negro
- ☐ American Indian or Alaska Native — *Print name of enrolled or principal tribe.* ⟋

- ☐ Asian Indian ☐ Japanese ☐ Native Hawaiian
- ☐ Chinese ☐ Korean ☐ Guamanian or Chamorro
- ☐ Filipino ☐ Vietnamese ☐ Samoan
- ☐ Other Asian — *Print race.* ⟋ ☐ Other Pacific Islander — *Print race.* ⟋

- ☐ Some other race — *Print race.* ⟋

→ **If more people live here, continue with Person 2.**

Form **D-61A**

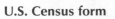

U.S. Census form

Migrations

For a wide variety of reasons, people have always been on the move from one place to another, a process known as migration. (Humans aren't the only ones who migrate; animals do the same thing, although not always for the same reasons!) The first migrants were our ancestors—nomadic **hunter-gatherers** who constantly were on the move to find the food they needed to keep alive. Scientists, geographers, and historians estimate that these hunter-gatherers originated in Africa 1.5 to 2 million years ago, evolved into *Homo sapiens* between two hundred thousand and three hundred thousand years ago, and then about fifty thousand years ago began to leave—migrate—from Africa to other parts of the world. It took about thirty thousand years for them to spread over Earth, settling in all the continents except Antarctica.

When we put the emphasis on where people came from before, we call them **emigrants.** When we place emphasis on where people now live, we call them **immigrants.** So we say, "Emigrants *from* England traveled on the *Mayflower*," or we say, "The immigrants *to* America traveled on the *Mayflower*."

Emigration and immigration can be understood in terms of a worldwide "push" and "pull" system. That is, emigrants leave their original homes because negative economic factors—lack of money, jobs, housing, educational opportunities—or political, religious, and social problems push them out. On the other side, the places they immigrate to pull, or attract, them with the hope of better jobs, housing, schools, religious toleration, full political rights, and so on.

Some people have not voluntarily emigrated. Millions of people have had to relocate because of slavery, a system that takes people from their homelands and sells them to work in another part of the world.

Nowadays, the human landscape of America continually changes—not only because of immigrants moving into the United States but also because of millions of people already here who migrate to another part of the country. Every year, about one out of six Americans moves—a little over 45 million people.

WHAT'S THE CONNECTION BETWEEN PLACE AND OCCUPATION?

Throughout history, *where* people live has, to some degree, determined what kind of work they do—and vice versa. Work that produces goods or services on a large scale is called an **industry. Technology** is the use of science to make industries more efficient. In our time, a huge number of people work in five industries.

Agriculture

As mentioned, learning to grow food was a key development in human history. And since the time, around 9000 B.C., when someone saw a connection between seeds and crops, many human beings living near fertile ground have continued to work in agriculture, which is the science of growing crops, raising livestock, and cultivating the soil. Some people have even taken infertile ground and, through much labor, converted it into fertile land.

Thousands of years ago, in addition to farming the land, people began to **domesticate**—that is, raise—previously wild animals for use by humans. Hunting dogs were the first domesticated animals. Then people began to raise sheep, goats, cattle, and pigs for milk, butter, cheese, meat, and hides; after many more years, people figured out how to use their cattle to pull their plows so that they could farm larger areas.

When agriculture started, a family or small group engaged in what is called **subsistence farming**—growing food and raising animals only for its members. Over the centuries, agriculture saw new tools and improved crops, but it wasn't until the twentieth century that the farm industry took really rapid strides. The development of mechanized farm equipment and the electrification of farms in various parts of the world caused an agricultural revolution, which heightened the yields of most farmers. Nowadays, we talk about **agribusiness**—farming on a huge scale.

One of the ways the farming business increased yields involved using new chemicals, including pesticides. Unfortunately, some of this progress also brought about negative results. For example, the chemicals sometimes upset the balance of nature by destroying some insects, animals, and plants that were actually helpful. Agricultural scientists are now looking into chemicals that will be not only effective but also safe.

Significant advances have also taken place in breeding. In previous centuries, farmers made new strains of plants and animals though trial-and-error breeding experiments. But in the past hundred years, as scientists and farmers came to understand better the workings of genes, they've more easily created new and more productive plants, seeds, and animals. These developments in turn have helped to increase the amount of food available to the world's population.

Most dramatically, for the past quarter century, scientists have been able to alter and add cells to produce healthier, stronger breeds; this process is called **genetic engineering.** As with pesticides, though, there is <u>controversy</u> surrounding this process; some people are concerned about the long-term effects of genetically engineered animals and crops on the people who eat them.

Can We Feed Everyone?

The challenge of feeding everyone has been less a production problem than a distribution problem—getting the food to people who are hungry. Some countries, like the United States, have had a tremendous amount of food, while others, like Bangladesh and Ethiopia, have struggled to deliver adequate food to their populations. Although statistics vary widely, many food experts estimate that about 10 percent of the world's population is hungry on a regular basis. Ending hunger will be one of the major challenges of the twenty-first century.

Fisheries

Just as people living on fertile land figured out how to use it to survive, so people living near water also found a livelihood related to their place. In the beginning, humans caught only enough fish, shellfish, and other water animals to feed themselves. Today, fishery is a big business. It involves not only catching and farming fish, shell-

fish, and other water animals but also the processing and selling of the product.

Fisheries are an especially important business in island nations such as Iceland and Japan, but in the last few decades the demand for fishery products has increased rapidly all over the world. In fact, scientists have warned that some fisheries—such as swordfish, bluefin tuna, and red snapper—are in decline; these scientists worry that other fish stocks will soon be in trouble, too.

This situation has led to farming fish, also called **aquaculture.** People in ancient China, India, and Egypt cultivated fish and shellfish. But now, in our day, aquaculture in tanks, lakes, ponds, and oceans is an exploding new part of the fishery business. For example, shrimp farming is important in parts of the American South, Latin America, and Asia.

Mining

One of the other major occupations and industries connected to a place is mining, the process of removing valuable materials from Earth. People have been mining for thousands of years, taking rocks, minerals, coal, sand, and other useful substances from the ground. Mining, like agriculture and fisheries, began with simple tools. In the last hundred years, modern technology has introduced complex machines and methods.

There are two major approaches to mining today: **surface mining** and **underground mining.** Surface mining refers to extracting resources that are close to or on the top of the ground. One example of surface mining is **strip mining,** which uses giant machines to cut away the top layer of Earth and expose coal that is located right under it. **Open-pit mining,** for minerals such as copper and iron, involves cutting huge holes in the ground to reveal minerals to be mined. **Quarrying,** another kind of surface mining, requires miners to cut large slabs of granite, sandstone, limestone, or marble out of the sides of huge pits dug in the ground.

Underground mining, on the other hand, requires digging deep into Earth to reach materials. This kind of mining involves creating shafts through which workers descend to dig out coal or minerals, which they then bring up to the surface. Modern technology has changed this type of mining somewhat; nowadays, machines do a great deal of the work, including some of the digging and much of the transporting of the coal or minerals. Other examples of underground mining include offshore oil rigs, which search for valuable deposits on land beneath the ocean.

Despite these advances, mining remains one of the most dangerous occupations in the world. Miners face the threat of fatal cave-ins and explosions; in addition, the years spent digging coal and other materials can lead to health problems. Miners have often formed **trade unions** to demand less dangerous working conditions. There's another problem related to mining, too: we're running out of some of the resources that we've been mining. The topic of conservation comes up later in the chapter.

Forestry

Forestry is the cultivation, maintenance, and cutting down of Earth's forests for wood, which we need for a wide variety of products. In the past, when the world's forests were abundant, people cut trees for use, and then the trees replaced themselves naturally. In more modern times, as demand for wood products has risen, tree farming has developed. Companies plant forests specifically to harvest them for commercial uses. Forestry's yield provides us with home-building materials, paper and cartons, medicines, furniture, gums, resins, waxes, charcoal, bats, hockey sticks, and pencils.

Manufacturing

Manufacturing means making new products from raw materials. (**Raw materials** are natural resources such as water or the items resulting from agriculture, fisheries, and mining.) Examples of manufacturing include preserving and canning agriculture and fishery products; converting trees into lumber for homes; and working with plant fibers to make fabrics—say, cotton cloth—and then making the fabrics into clothing. These days, manufacturing also refers to making new products from recycled materials.

At first, people manufactured things only by hand and only for themselves; this manufacturing took place in people's homes. Then people started manufacturing things for one another, and the manufacturing still took place in people's homes. Beginning in the 1700s, inventors designed machines—such as the steam engine—that made manufacturing easier, quicker, and cheaper.

With the appearance of machines, manufacturers got involved in **mass production**—manufacturing many items at a time rather than only one at a time. At this point, the elements of manufacturing—the raw materials, the workers, and the machines—moved into mills and factories.

Since manufacturers needed energy to run their machines, they set up the first mills and factories near waterfalls and rapids. Manufacturers built waterwheels over which the falls and rapids fell, providing energy to run machinery. Manufacturers also had to put their mills and factories near rivers and railroads so that they could receive the other natural resources they needed, as well as ship out their finished products. Once other sources of energy—such as electricity—became available, manufacturers weren't as tied down to a specific place.

Other Ways to Earn a Living

Not everyone in the world is a farmer, fisher, miner, logger, or manufacturer. Much of the rest of the world's population provides services to these industries—everything from accounting to communications to legal services to vacation planning. People in these service industries are not so dependent on geography. In fact, they may live and work in several different regions in the course of their lifetimes.

The Information Age

In the last part of the twentieth century and the beginning of the twenty-first, much of the world witnessed a dramatic change in culture and lifestyle as technological developments—computers, faxes, cellular phones, and the Internet—changed life forever. The world had been in the Industrial Age since the opening of the first mills in England in the eighteenth century. In very recent history, the world has entered the Information Age. Where people live does not limit the kind of work they do as much as in the past. When someone in Seattle is having trouble with his or her computer and calls a help line, the person answering (in English) and solving the problem may be in Washington State . . . or India.

Trade Moves All These Products

Because not everyone lives next to a farm, ocean, forest, factory, or mine, a system of buying, selling, and distributing products has developed. This is the world's network of trade—the exchange of goods and services among Earth's people.

Trade initially was the exchange of one product for another: someone gave a fish to another person in return for a piece of meat, for example. When no money is used to transact the exchange, as in this example, the process is known as **barter.** Barter was the predominant form of trade for many centuries, until money altered how people did business. They began paying for, rather than bartering for, goods and services.

Controlling trade among people and countries has led to both progress and conflict for societies for thousands of years. As we saw earlier, in Chapter 1, Marco Polo's explorations of and writing about the East led to increased overland trade between Europe and Asia in the late Middle Ages and then, starting in the fifteenth century, spurred the search for sea routes. Battles for control of the sea—and trade—became common. Later, there were fights about railroads and, later still, about which countries could fly to and land in other countries.

Today, diplomats generate many agreements among countries to control the terms of trade; for example, NAFTA—the North American Free Trade Agreement—came into being in the 1990s to reduce or end taxes on goods traveling between the United States, Canada, and Mexico. The goal was increased trade.

The issue of **globalization** comes up in any discussion of modern-day international trade. On one level, globalization simply means we use products from all over the world, just as things made in the United States go to countries all over the globe. However, globalization sometimes means decision making by international groups or businesses rather than by individual countries.

Supporters of globalization argue that some challenges (for example, poverty, hunger, and working conditions) are too large for individual nations to handle, so they suggest more cooperation between nations. On the other hand, protesters against globalization fear that as countries become more connected by trade, people will no longer identify with individual nations. Others protest that corporations rather than nations are becoming too strong.

HOW SHOULD PEOPLE TREAT EARTH?

The issue of globalization also comes up when talking about natural resources. Can all nations agree on how to treat Earth?

Today the challenge of protecting natural resources is greater than ever because of the tremendous potential—positive and negative—of technology, coupled with the strains produced by the expanding population. **Conservation** is the responsible use of natural resources, ensuring that people can use them now and in the future.

The needs and desires of a region's people may collide with those of a corporation; for example, Company X may want to dig for oil off the coast of a small community, but accidents such as oil spills from drilling may negatively affect the inhabitants of the community—human, animal, and fish. Or Factory Y may be manufacturing needed products but polluting the environment in the process.

The study of the interaction among all the living things and their environment is known as **ecology.** Ecologists have suggested more effective and responsible means of using Earth's resources. For example, they propose farming techniques that contribute to soil conservation; they suggest that foresters cut trees prudently rather than practice **clear-cutting,** which wipes out whole areas of forests and leads to the loss of topsoil; they design recycling programs to reduce demands for more paper and other products; they call for reducing acid rain, fallout that comes from factories and hurts the environment; and they advise less use of transportation dependent on oil. The problem is that sometimes programs such as those just listed cost a lot of money for individuals, businesses, or governments and cause a lot of inconvenience. The search for fair solutions must go on.

If We Can't Control Nature, What Can We Do?

Humans have witnessed nature's awesome power throughout history, and modern societies are not immune to natural disasters.

Avalanches

An avalanche occurs when a mass of snow, rocks, or other material is dislodged and quickly flows down the side of a mountain. A number of events can trigger an avalanche: an earthquake, heavy snowfall, vibrations caused by skiers, or a sudden temperature change. In Peru, in 1970, a deadly avalanche blanketed the town of Yungay, killing over sixteen thousand people.

Cyclones, Hurricanes, and Typhoons

All three of these terms apply to violent storms involving powerful, twisting winds, centered around the "eye" of the storm. The term *hurricane* is used for a storm originating in the Caribbean, Atlantic Ocean, Gulf of Mexico, or eastern Pacific; *typhoon* refers to a similar storm in the western Pacific Ocean, especially the South China Sea; and *cyclone* is the name given to storms in the northern Indian Ocean and the Bay of Bengal. These rotating tropical storms have winds that are stronger than 74 miles an hour (119 kilometers an hour). Even more deadly than the winds is the storm's effect on the ocean: waves can rise more than 25 feet (7.6 meters) above the level of the ocean and can lead to many drowning deaths.

Tornadoes

A tornado, also known as a twister, is a form of a cyclone over land. It involves a violent twisting column of air that extends down to the land from a storm cloud. The average tornado is about 600 feet (183 meters) wide and moves at about 30 miles an hour (48 kilometers an hour) but can go up to 70 miles an hour (113 kilometers an hour). A tornado's winds are much more powerful than a sea-based cyclone's; estimates reach as high as 300 miles an hour (483 kilometers an hour; no one knows a definite maximum speed since no instruments can hold up to the tornado's force!).

Tsunamis

Tsunamis are powerful ocean waves that surge onto shore, especially in the Pacific region. They are triggered by earthquakes or volcanoes, which have occurred in or near the ocean. Tsunamis can move at speeds up to 500 miles an hour (805 kilometers an hour); when they hit the shore, they can produce tremendous destruction due to their one-hundred-foot-high (thirty-meter-high) waves and speed.

Floods and Droughts

A flood is an overflowing of water on land that normally is not covered by water. In addition to resulting from tsunamis, floods come about from excessive rainfall that swells rivers, lakes, and oceans and from rainfall on a land surface that is too dry to absorb it. A flash flood is a sudden rise due to heavy rainfall; a coastal flood, usually caused by tropical storms, can create disastrous conditions for the coast's inhabitants; a seasonal flood occurs on a regular basis and may actually be beneficial to certain land.

At the opposite end of the disaster spectrum is a drought, which is a long period without any—or with hardly any—precipitation. A drought may last a few weeks, termed *dry spells*, or can endure for months and even years. Droughts affect more people globally than any other natural disaster; perhaps the worst recorded in history was in China in the 1870s, when more than 10 million people died because of the lack of rain. There is no single cause of droughts; a variety of conditions combine to produce the shortage in precipitation.

One of the related problems of a drought or flood can be **famine,** which is an extreme shortage of food in a region over an extended period of time. Famines can result from floods or droughts that make it impossible to harvest crops, from destruction of crops by insects or diseases, and from wars that interfere with farmers' work.

Surviving a Natural Disaster

In some ways, we are better equipped to deal with natural disasters now; advances in weather forecasting and disaster planning make it possible to avoid some aspects of nature's fury, and recovery and relief may be quicker and more effective than in the past.

People who have practiced emergency drills and who heed local authorities are more likely to survive than those who take foolish chances.

! Implications

To answer the question, "Why does all this matter?" or "What does it mean?," share the following insights with your child.

This chapter raises seven questions about people's lives on Earth. The first two—What's in a culture? and How did civilizations develop?— already have relatively agreed-upon answers and, outside of school, may not be asked very often. But the next five questions will keep coming up during our lifetimes:

- How many people are there?
- Where do people live?
- What's the connection between place and occupation?
- How should people treat Earth?
- If we can't control nature, what *can* we do to survive?

Over time, the answers to those five questions will change. Change, as never before, is the only constant—at least in this country.

Change in America, in fact, is probably the major theme of this chapter. If we had lived here ten thousand years ago, our chances of running into people from another culture and of experiencing any significant change from one day to the next (other than changes in the weather and in the condition of our bodies) would have been slim. Today, though, we in America are always running into— sometimes colliding with—different cultures, and, as a result, we change and change again. This year can be totally different from last year for us, as we meet new challenges on the national level and as we change what we wear, what we eat, and where we travel, individually.

At the same time, as life keeps speeding up and changing in America, we need to remember that in some other countries people simply have not known change the way we have. In some countries, life is not much different for people today from what it was for their ancestors, hundreds of years ago. They still face a daily struggle for existence.

So, for this chapter, we come to a final pair of questions: Are there changes that can be good for us, good for people in other countries, *and* at the same time good for Earth? How can we make those changes happen?

✔ *Fact Checker*

To check that your child knows or can find the basic facts in this chapter, here is a puzzle based on this chapter.

PEOPLE AND EARTH PUZZLE

Across

6. agent that kills insects
8. responsible use of resources
9. opposite of emigrant
10. water, air, and soil (2 words)

Down

1. name of issue with pros and cons
2. growing and cutting down trees
3. long dry spell
4. trade without money
5. violent storm
7. person who compiles people statistics

Answers appear in the back, preceding the index.

? The Big Questions

The following questions encourage your child to think critically rather than simply recall facts. If necessary, review the specific information from the preceding pages that will help your child make the necessary inferences to come up with reasonable answers.

1. Select one culture that you belong to, and describe what's special about it. You may comment on any of the following parts of the culture: language, belief systems, customs, food, clothing, government, and attitudes toward natural surroundings.
2. If you could choose to live your teenage years in a city, a suburb, or a rural location, which would you choose? Why?
3. Would you rather celebrate your birthday with a homemade birthday cake or a store-bought one? Why?

Suggested Answers

1. *Your child may answer this question in terms of a nationality, ethnic group, or religion that he or she belongs to. Alternatively, he or she may choose to discuss the culture of people in his or her age group.*
2. *Encourage your child to answer in terms of advantages (or disadvantages) of each locale. Your child might comment, for example, on safety, schools, mix of people, local activities, population density, access to nature, and so on.*
3. *Your child might acknowledge the personal effort that goes into a homemade cake and its potential to stand out from the ordinary. On the other hand, your child might say he or she prefers the mass-produced cake because it may look more professional. (The same question can be asked about homemade clothes versus store-bought ones.)*

Skills Practice

The following activities give your child practice in applying the skills basic to social studies. For some of the activities, your child may need to review the information in the preceding pages.

A. DISTINGUISHING FACT FROM OPINION

Review with your child the definitions of the words *fact* and *opinion*. Establish that statements of fact can be checked to find out whether they are true or false, while statements of opinion are neither true nor false—they represent the judgments people have made. Then ask your child to identify the following statements as facts or opinions. Encourage your child to explain each identification.

1. There are too many people on Earth.
2. Ancient Chinese civilization was better than ancient Egyptian civilization.
3. Another name for a tornado is twister.
4. Tsunamis can travel as fast as five hundred miles an hour (805 kilometers an hour).
5. Globalization is bad for Canadians.

Answers

1. opinion; 2. opinion; 3. fact; 4. fact; 5. opinion

Evaluating Your Child's Skills: In order to complete this activity successfully, your child needs to understand that a fact is a statement that can be shown to be true or false. An opinion cannot be true or false because it states a judgment that an individual person has made. If your child has trouble, point out key words and phrases that are typical in statements of opinion: *too many, better than, bad.*

B. CONDUCTING A CENSUS FOR AGE

> This activity involves calling on your neighbors. Based on your community, you may want to slip an announcement about your child's project under people's doors a few days before you start ringing doorbells.

Conduct a census by asking each neighbor how many people live in his or her home and how old each person is. You may conduct your census on one or more floors of an apartment building or in the houses on one or both sides of a block. If you live far away from other people, you may phone neighbors in the vicinity to ask your questions. Here's some general advice.

1. Set up a data-collection form on which to record, for each home, the number of inhabitants and the age of each person.
2. Photocopy the form so that you have one for each home you visit or call.
3. Use age ranges such as "under 1," "2–5," "6–10," and so on. The upper ranges can be "30–39," "40–49," up to "90 or older."
4. Be polite to people who prefer not to answer your questions.
5. Figure out what to do with your data. Can you make a generalization about the ages of people in nearby families? Can you make a graph to show the age ranges that most of the people fall into? Will you tell your neighbors what you found?

> *Evaluating Your Child's Skills:* In order to complete this activity successfully, your child will be using organizational skills, interpersonal skills, and mathematics or reasoning skills. Help your child realize that when doing such a project for the first time, people cannot anticipate every development. Stress that your child can modify his or her approach along the way.

C. BRAINSTORMING: CONSERVATION AT HOME

> Work with your child to think of ways to conserve resources beyond what your family does at home now. Brainstorming together is often more productive than brainstorming alone.

Brainstorm additional ways your family can save water, electricity, and trees. When you've run out of ideas, look over your list. Select three ideas that you like, and propose them to the other members of your family to vote on.

Put the winning idea into practice. After some time passes, meet with the other members of your family to discuss what you've accomplished or what you need to change about the new policy.

> *Evaluating Your Child's Skills:* In order to complete this activity successfully, your child needs to understand that brainstorming involves taking chances. Even if an idea sounds weak (or worse), mentioning it may help someone else in the brainstorming group come up with a good idea. If your child has trouble coming up with ideas, suggest that he or she think about the following:
>
> *To save water*
> **Laundry and dishes**
> **New plants**
> *To save electricity*
> **Candlelight**
> **Fan in combination with air conditioner**
> *To save trees*
> **Greeting cards and envelopes**
> **Paper towels and dinner napkins**

☆ # Top of the Class

> Children interested in delving more deeply into the topics covered in this chapter can

choose one or more of the following activities. They may do the activities for their own satisfaction or report on what they have done to show that they have been seriously considering the effects Earth and people have on each other.

INTERVIEWING

Arrange to have your child interview someone who can shed personal light on one of the following experiences mentioned in this chapter: (1) immigrating to the United States from somewhere else; (2) surviving a natural disaster.

As you prepare for and conduct your interview, keep in mind that your interviewee may have very strong feelings about his or her experience. If the interviewee seems uncomfortable with a question of yours, politely withdraw the question, and move on to another one. With the person's permission, you might tape the interview and present it in class.

CONSULTING EXPERTS

Introduce your child to the following Web site: www.hurricanehunters.com. This site, which belongs to the Hurricane Hunters Association, provides a huge amount of up-to-the-minute information, gathered firsthand; in spite of its "com" suffix, the site sells absolutely nothing.

Travel around www.hurricanehunters.com to figure out which parts of the site you find most useful or fascinating. Check on the short movies, the "Cyberflight into the Eye" feature, the question-and-answer section, and anything else that catches your attention. Consider sending the address of the site

to your teacher or to classmates. Include a note about why you recommend the site.

Then perhaps the students, working cooperatively, can submit to this site a single question about hurricanes.

WORKING WITH LITERATURE AND ART

The following activity will work with many other picture books that tell about extreme weather conditions. The activity specifically focuses on a picture book for younger children so that your child has the opportunity to evaluate not just a story but art as well.

The book *Drylongso* was written by Virginia Hamilton and illustrated by Jerry Pinkney (Harcourt, 1992). It is available in libraries and bookstores—perhaps in the children's room. (The publisher and reviewers say the book is for children younger than you, but many older children and adults like to read it.) After you read the book, consider the following questions and the suggestion that follows them.

1. What bad weather condition do the characters find themselves in at the beginning of the book?
2. Do the characters survive? How?
3. Tell what you like or don't like about the illustrations in the book. Tell why you think the illustrations are or are not right for the story.

Suggestion

Illustrate a scene from the book yourself. It may be a scene already illustrated in the book, or it may be a scene not illustrated in the book. When you're finished, be prepared to tell why you used the same colors that the illustrator uses in this book or different colors.

CHAPTER 6
Geography of the United States by Regions

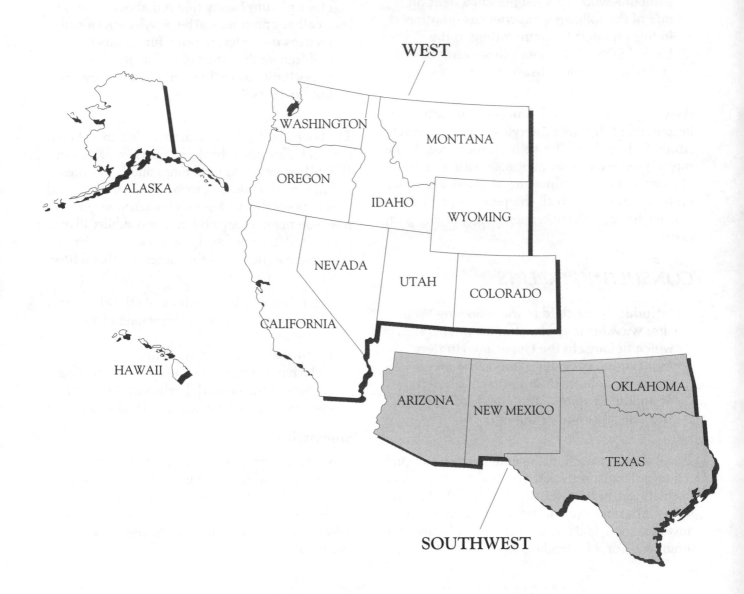

WEST

ALASKA

WASHINGTON

MONTANA

OREGON

IDAHO

WYOMING

HAWAII

NEVADA

UTAH

COLORADO

CALIFORNIA

ARIZONA

NEW MEXICO

OKLAHOMA

TEXAS

SOUTHWEST

Regions are areas with common characteristics that distinguish them from other areas. A region can be as small as a neighborhood or as vast as the American West. Ways to designate regions range from cultural criteria such as language to political criteria such as type of government to physical criteria such as nearness. This chapter explores two ways that we can classify the regions of the United States—first by groups of states, as illustrated by the "jigsaw" map here, and then by dominant physical traits, as illustrated by the "United States: Physical" map in the atlas at the back of the book.

MIDDLE WEST

MID-ATLANTIC

NEW ENGLAND

NORTH DAKOTA

MINNESOTA

NEW HAMPSHIRE

VERMONT

MAINE

WISCONSIN

MICHIGAN

NEW YORK

MASSACHUSETTS

SOUTH DAKOTA

RHODE ISLAND
CONNECTICUT

IOWA

INDIANA

OHIO

PENNSYLVANIA

NEBRASKA

ILLINOIS

NEW JERSEY

DELAWARE

MARYLAND

KANSAS

MISSOURI

WEST VIRGINIA

VIRGINIA

KENTUCKY

NORTH CAROLINA

TENNESSEE

SOUTH CAROLINA

ARKANSAS

MISSISSIPPI

ALABAMA

GEORGIA

LOUISIANA

FLORIDA

SOUTHEAST

Word Power

The words on the following chart are underscored in the section called "What Your Child Needs to Know." Explain their meanings to your child as necessary when the words come up in reading or discussion. Keep this list handy for you and your child to use.

Word	*Definition*
blighted	destroyed
bogs	wet, spongy land
continental	referring to a continent (The continental United States is the forty-eight adjoining states.)
dominant	most influential or powerful
economy	set of arrangements by which a group of people or a nation produces and distributes the goods and services needed by the people
feudal	referring to a system in which people who worked an owner's land and fought for the owner received land and protection from him or her
flanked	guarded
fragile	delicate
metropolis	a large city or center of population and culture
retire	end a career or stop going to a daily job
variety	number of different things
visualize	picture something in one's mind

What Your Child Needs to Know

You may choose to use the following text in several different ways, depending on your child's strengths and preferences. You might read the passage aloud; you might read it to yourself and then paraphrase it for your child; or you might ask your child to read the material along with you or on his or her own.

INTRODUCTION TO U.S. REGIONS

When people picture the United States, they may <u>visualize</u> a map in the familiar shape of the country. Or they may see a collection of snapshots that, put together, capture the country's <u>variety</u> over its 3,717,796 square miles (9,628,348 square kilometers). That number, by the way, makes the United States the fourth-largest country in the world in land area.

If we took a journey across this vast land, we would discover snow-clad mountains, fields of grain, scorching sandy deserts, rocky canyons, great lakes, and powerful rivers. In many parts of the country, we'd also come across huge cities, but we'd find smaller towns or suburbs all over the United States, too.

LOOKING AT THE COUNTRY AS GROUPS OF STATES

How can we get to know the variety of the United States without examining each of the fifty states one by one? We'll look at states that are near one another as a *group of connected states*. In other words, we'll look at regions of the country. (The chapter-opening pages explain that people have different ways of identifying regions. Right now when we say *region*, we mean "states that are near one another and form a group.") Specifically, we'll look at six regions and then at two states that are off on their own, physically speaking. Here are a preview of how we name the regions and a list of the states in each group. Fuller discussion follows.

Region	States in Region
New England	Connecticut, Maine, Massachusetts, New Hampshire, Rhode Island, Vermont
Mid-Atlantic	Delaware, Maryland, New Jersey, New York, Pennsylvania
Southeast	Alabama, Arkansas, Florida, Georgia, Kentucky, Louisiana, Mississippi, North Carolina, South Carolina, Tennessee, Virginia, West Virginia
Midwest	Illinois, Indiana, Iowa, Kansas, Michigan, Minnesota, Missouri, Nebraska, North Dakota, Ohio, South Dakota, Wisconsin
Southwest	Arizona, New Mexico, Oklahoma, Texas

West
   Mountain West
   California
   Northwest
	
	Colorado, Idaho, Montana, Nevada, Utah, Wyoming
	California
	Oregon, Washington

Separate states	Alaska, Hawaii

New England

Where can we spy the first orange leaves of autumn, ski down a spectacular slope, and watch whales play in the ocean? We can enjoy all of these activities in the New England region.

During the ice age that ended about nine or ten thousand years ago, glaciers sculptured the New England landscape, dumping boulders and forming sand dunes. Perhaps one of the rocks deposited by a glacier is Plymouth Rock, in Massachusetts, where the Pilgrims came ashore to settle in 1620.

The rocky land and harsh winter made life difficult for these early settlers. *Wampanoag* (*wahm puh NOH ag*) tribes helped New Englanders harvest crops and fish. Soon settlers spread out across New England; they cut the forests and farmed the land. Others settled near harbors dotting the Atlantic coast and waterways such as the Connecticut River. Boston's harbor played a role in the days leading up to the Revolutionary War and is still important today.

Water is a great resource and the key to many other resources in New England. Harvesting cranberries in <u>bogs</u> for Thanksgiving dinner, growing wild blueberries and sugar maples for blueberry pancakes with syrup, and raising dairy cattle for ice cream all require water.

To this day, like Native Americans before them, New Englanders catch lobster in the Atlantic Ocean off the coast of Maine and dig up clams in Massachusetts. Water also attracts visitors, who splash in the Cape Cod surf and ski the slopes of Vermont's Green Mountains or New Hampshire's White Mountains. And the right amount of rainfall leads to a colorful show of fall foliage.

Water power also had a role in shaping the New England <u>economy</u>. Factories harnessed the power in rivers and streams to help machines churn out items during the Industrial Revolution. New England factory workers mass-produced everything from clocks to textiles to muskets. When manufacturing moved to the southern United States and overseas, many New Englanders began to work in different jobs, such as tourism and other fields providing services to customers. Today New Englanders find a mixture of careers among their neighbors—professors, innkeepers, insurance representatives, magazine editors, and farmers growing produce for gourmet restaurants in Boston.

About 13,900,000 people call New England home, according to the 2000 census figures. Most of the population lives in big cities like Boston, Massachusetts; Portland, Maine; and Bridgeport, Connecticut.

A final note: it was Captain John Smith, an Englishman who had been active in the southern colony of Jamestown, Virginia, who began to call this region New England.

Mid-Atlantic

Approximately in the middle of the country's east coast, the mid-Atlantic region consists of five states, four of which have seashores. So some people in the region turn to the sea to make their living. While the Native Americans fished in dugout canoes, fishers today cast their nets into the Atlantic Ocean from ships of all sizes. Then the fish is prepared and packed in ice, loaded on trucks, and shipped to fish distribution centers such as the Fulton Fish Market in New York City, where it is sold to restaurant chefs and fish stores.

Besides being a source of food, the Atlantic along these states provides deep harbors. So ships carrying goods from all over the world anchor in New York City, Philadelphia, and other east coast ports. When the Erie Canal opened in 1825, this 363-mile (584-kilometer) waterway connected Lake Erie and the Hudson River; in other words, the canal provided a link between the Great Lakes and the Atlantic Ocean. Its use declined when railroads and highways began to crisscross the mid-Atlantic states.

Sandy soils and the long growing seasons in a climate milder than New England's form the perfect combination for crops such as potatoes, sweet corn, and tomatoes. In the Pennsylvania Dutch region, Amish farmers raise tobacco using old European farming methods. The Niagara Fruit Belt, near the Great Lakes, contains apple, peach, and plum orchards.

In addition to the ocean and good soil, the mid-Atlantic region has mountains. On a helicopter journey from northern New York State down to Maryland, we would spy many mountain ranges towering above the region. Hikers and skiers scale the peaks of the Catskills, the Adirondacks, the Blue Ridge, and the Appalachian mountains.

At some moments during a helicopter ride, towering business and residential structures rather than mountains would catch our attention. Mighty skyscrapers sometimes seem to crowd out the sun in huge mid-Atlantic cities such as New York, Newark, Philadelphia, and Baltimore.

About 45,800,000 people live in the mid-Atlantic states, with the highest numbers in the cities, of course. For example, in New York City there are approximately 66,835 people per square mile, while in the state overall there are 402 people per square mile.

Steel was once the backbone of many mid-Atlantic cities, such as Pittsburgh, which is now home to research industries. The New Jersey area contains headquarters for many pharmaceutical companies, while New York City is considered the United States's finance, fashion, publishing, and theater center.

Two Other Labels

Some books talk about New England and the mid-Atlantic together and call the combined area the Northeast. Another label used when talking about this area is *BosWash*—a name made up by combining the first syllable of Boston with the first syllable of Washington, D.C. The name comes about because there is so much population between these two cities that it sometimes seems as if it's one big metropolis.

Southeast

In the Old South of the nineteenth century, cotton reigned as king of the crops. The hot, humid weather, rich soil, and flat land had earlier supported other crops, such as rice and tobacco. However, after the 1793 invention of the cotton gin, which separated seeds from cotton, the product took off on a major scale throughout the South. Large land estates called **plantations** imported slaves from Africa to work the cotton fields just as they previously worked tobacco and rice fields.

In 1865, at the end of the Civil War, American slaves were granted their freedom. Many continued to work in the cotton belt as tenant farmers, renting land from plantation owners. But then a tiny insect toppled the cotton empire. Boll weevils crossed the Rio Grande from Mexico in 1892, chomping their way through cotton pods. They destroyed a large portion of the region's cotton crops.

Up from the blighted fields of the Old South rose the New South. A new series of crops—peanuts, oranges, grapefruit, and sweet potatoes—replaced cotton. But the promise of higher salaries for less labor-intensive work in manufacturing lured a steady stream of people from farms to cities such as Atlanta, Georgia. And while North Carolina continues to lead the United States in tobacco production, it has moved into other fields, such as high-tech manufacturing in the Research Triangle complex near Chapel Hill.

The U.S. government spurred development in the Southeast. For example, the Tennessee Valley Authority helped the region to grow by building dams that rerouted water and converted the water power to low-cost electricity. Area industries ranging from health care, textiles, and retailer headquarters to small-business support systems depend on this electricity.

The year-round sunshine of the Southeast attracts visitors, many of whom later retire in this sun belt. Like **Juan Ponce de León** (WAN POHN say day lay OHN), who journeyed to Florida in 1513 in search of the legendary Fountain of Youth, vacationers have discovered the New South.

Overpopulation has caused problems in this region. The twelve Southeastern states contain approximately 69,300,000 people, with population growing by leaps and bounds in each state. In Florida, where the population rose 24 percent in the last ten years to about 15,982,000 people in the year 2000, fragile wetlands were being damaged by development and pollution. The swamps and marshes of the Everglades and Big Cypress Swamp, which help control flooding and provide shelter for the threatened Florida panther, are now under protection.

The busy international port of New Orleans ships Louisiana's main crops—sweet potatoes, sugarcane, and pecans—along with oil from offshore deposits in the Gulf of Mexico. The city of New Orleans hosts a Mardi Gras carnival in its French Quarter. The city was the birthplace of jazz musician **Louis "Satchmo" Armstrong,** and music ranging from jazz to the blues pours out of this region day and night, especially during festivals, while, farther north in Nashville, Tennessee, country music dominates.

(Some books go on to discuss the Commonwealth of Puerto Rico when covering the Southeast, but this book is concentrating on the fifty states.)

Midwest

The twelve midwestern states, six clustered between the Ohio River and the Great Lakes and six farther west, are sometimes described as the breadbasket of America. In the heartland, or center, of the United States, the flat plains once were home to prairie grass. Early settlers discovered that corn, wheat, and oats grew quickly in the rich soil, and soon these grains replaced much of the grass. As noted, after the Erie Canal opened in 1825, these grains were shipped to New York and ground into flour for bread. Now bushels of wheat travel from midwestern bins to markets by railways and trucks.

Other farmers raised livestock, such as sheep, pigs, and beef cattle. Wisconsin earned its reputation as America's dairyland because of all the milk, butter, and cheese produced from dairy cows that graze on the prairies. Times change, and, today, small family farms have given way to giant farming corporations.

Along with farms, manufacturing towns sprouted in the Midwest. Factories churned out products that were shipped around the world. Steel plants opened in the Great Lakes area and soon supplied raw materials for the new automobile industry in Detroit, Michigan, where, along the way, robots began to perform jobs people once held. Factories in Chicago, Illinois, packaged meat. Those in Milwaukee made machinery.

Many of these midwestern states have reinvented themselves. That is, they've changed their focus from agriculture to industry and high-tech work in microbiology and computers. Wisconsin, for example, has moved beyond dairy to host industries such as motorcycle production, and today it is headquarters for an enormous diagnostic-imaging-equipment company.

The Midwest is home to about 64.4 million people. Several of America's largest cities are in this region, with almost 3 million people in Chicago and both Detroit and Cleveland going beyond 1 million.

We used to call this region the rust belt because it was so dependent on manufacturing. The region lost a lot of people when its manufacturers relocated to the sun belt, overseas, and to Mexico. More recently, as some cities expanded into research and development, both their economies and their populations have risen.

Southwest

The semiarid, or almost dry, land of the Southwest resembles a moon landscape in places, with plateaus and valleys, mesas and buttes. Long ago, Native Americans dwelling in this region mixed straw, clay, and dirt to form adobe bricks. They built pueblos, or villages, on top of the rocky mesas or into sides of cliffs by laying adobe bricks five stories high. Attached buildings made from these bricks sheltered many families. Since some buildings lacked doors, people entered by ladders leading to openings in the roofs.

The powerful Colorado River, which starts in the Rockies, carved the 2-billion-year-old Grand Canyon. This 277-mile (446-kilometer) gorge cuts through the Colorado Plateau, extending from the mouth of the Paria River in northern Arizona to Grand Wash Cliffs near the Nevada boundary. Tourists can examine the sculptured shapes and layers of colors up close if they walk or ride a mule down the canyon trail.

Native Americans grew maize (Indian corn), squash, and gourds in the Southwest. They shaped clay into pottery and raised sheep with long wool for weaving rugs and blankets. When Spaniards arrived in the region in the sixteenth century, they planted wheat and fruit trees and traveled on horses. Later, in the 1800s, another group joined the Native Americans and the Spaniards—people traveling west from the eastern United States.

Some people hoped to strike it rich in the Southwest. Although European explorers had searched the Southwest unsuccessfully for the imaginary Seven Cities of Gold, the area does really have a wealth of minerals. Arizona produces half of America's copper. New Mexico has supplies of uranium, potassium salts, gold, silver, and zinc. Texas is famous for its oil fields.

Native Americans continue to live in the Southwest, and most Native Americans in the region still rely on the land's natural resources. For example, the Navajo harvest natural gas, uranium, coal, and petroleum. And today the ground blossoms with a variety of crops, thanks to irrigation by rivers such as the Platte in Texas.

In 2000, the four states making up the Southwest had a combined population of about 31,300,000, with almost 20,900,000 residents in Texas. Large cities in this region include Houston, Dallas, Tulsa, Santa Fe, and Tucson.

West

We can break the West down into three subregions: California, the Mountain West, and the Pacific Northwest.

People raced to California after someone discovered gold at Sutter's Mill in 1848. Now more people (approximately 33,900,000) live here than in any other state, and supporters say that there's something for everyone in the Golden State. The Pacific Ocean borders the west coast, with beaches famous for surfing. Snowcapped Mount Whitney, highest in the continental United States at 14,494 feet (4,418 meters), contrasts with scorching Death Valley 282 feet (86 meters) below sea level, the lowest point in the country.

The active Lassen Peak volcano and San Andreas Fault are sources of possible natural disasters. Movement along the fault has indeed caused earthquakes.

While miners still find gold in California, other industries form the core of its economy. This state leads the nation in growing fruits and vegetables such as broccoli, carrots, lettuce, tomatoes, and strawberries and in producing wine and dairy products. Silicon Valley, between Palo Alto and San Jose, is the nation's leading producer of the semiconductors used in computers and other electronic appliances. And Hollywood is synonymous with the film and television industries.

The Mountain West contains about one-quarter of the land in the United States, and about 11,200,000 people call the Mountain West home. Rugged mountain ranges twist through all six states in the region. These include the Rockies, the Sierra Nevada, the Cascade Range, and the Pacific Coast Ranges.

Another natural wonder of the Mountain West is the Great Salt Lake of Utah. With more than 6 billion tons of salts, this lake is saltier than the ocean. Although nothing grows in the Bonneville Salt Flats to the west of the lake, an international auto raceway, the Bonneville Salt Flats Speedway, sees land speed records set.

Farther northwest, in Oregon and Washington, the thick forests and teeming waterways continue to produce. Native Americans living in the Pacific Northwest once carved totem poles and canoes from trees. They fished the streams and oceans and held special ceremonies to honor the salmon. Today, this region produces lumber, wood products, and paper, and contains one of the top salmon-fishing industries in the world.

About 9,315,000 reside in the Northwest. Key cities in these two areas—the Mountain West and the Northwest—include Salt Lake City, Denver, Las Vegas, Portland (Oregon), and Seattle.

Alaska

Called the Last Frontier because of its isolated location near the Arctic Circle, the area of Alaska is equal to one-fifth the area of the continental United States. The United States bought this largely unexplored chunk of land from the Russians in 1867 for about two cents an acre. The frozen region of glaciers and lakes had yet to be fully explored.

With the gold rush of 1898, more than thirty thousand people poured into Alaska. Since then, other natural riches hidden beneath the frozen earth have attracted exploration. When geologists discovered oil and gas in Prudhoe Bay on the Arctic Coast, workers built the Trans-Alaska Pipeline to carry these natural resources to the port of Valdez, from which they are shipped worldwide.

Other people enjoy Alaska's natural beauty and hunting and fishing opportunities. With more than a hundred state parks, there's a lot of territory to cover. A good place to start is Alaska's center, which marks the highest point in North America: Mount McKinley, soaring to a height of 20,320 feet (6,194 meters). Surrounding the mountain is Denali (duh NAH lee) National Park, where families of wolves roam in search of caribou. Volcanoes are active in the Valley of Ten Thousand Smokes at Katmai National Park, at the northern end of the Alaska peninsula. North America's longest glacier—the Bering Glacier—measures 127 miles (204 kilometers) long.

Some people in Alaska still travel by dogsled. New methods of transportation have linked remote villages to large cities such as Anchorage. Snowmobiles and all-terrain vehicles zip along snowy trails. Even once-unreachable areas receive mail and supplies from bush pilots who sometimes land their small planes on glaciers.

The 2000 population figure for Alaska was 627,000.

Hawaii

Far out in the Pacific Ocean, beginning about 2,400 miles (3,862 kilometers) southwest of the California coast, 130 tropical islands form the fiftieth state. Volcanoes rose from the ocean to create the 1,523-mile (2,451-kilometer) chain of islets and eight main islands of Hawaii. Towering above beaches fringed with palm trees, volcanoes such as Mauna Loa (*mow* nuh LOH uh) continue to erupt.

Rich volcanic soil and a tropical climate combine to create the perfect environment for orchids and other magnificent flowers, as well as such crops as sugarcane, pineapples, bananas, and macadamia nuts. The coffee belt in the Kona (KOH nuh) district, along the western coast of the island of Hawaii, is the only place in the United States where coffee grows.

Polynesians traveled in canoes from other Pacific islands to settle Hawaii. Descendants of these Polynesian voyagers formed their own island kingdom. Still standing today is Iolani, once the royal palace where Hawaii's last two monarchs ruled toward the end of the nineteenth century, before Hawaii gained statehood.

Europeans first visited the islands in 1778. At that time, James Cook, a British explorer popularly called Captain Cook, named them the Sandwich Islands in honor of the Earl of Sandwich. When Hawaii's <u>feudal</u> land system ended in 1848, other foreigners soon arrived, lured by the growing sugar trade. Newcomers continue to visit the islands, where they play in the tropical sun on 283 beaches.

At Honolulu's Waikiki Beach on the island of Oahu (oh AH *hoo*), surfers catch giant waves, and snorkelers explore lagoons, while other natives and tourists, from the safety of a charter boat, spot blacktip reef shark hunting in the coral. Rising in the background, the extinct volcano Diamond Head was once the home of the Fire Goddess. Nobody will discover diamonds littering the beaches, however. What the early explorers thought were diamonds turned out to be rock crystals.

The 2000 population count of Hawaii was 1,200,000.

LOOKING AT THE COUNTRY AS LANDFORMS

As the chapter opener mentions, breaking the United States down into groups of states—focusing on what neighboring states have in common—is only one way to divide the country into regions. Another way is to focus on <u>dominant</u> features of the land, features that may cut across two or more of the regions we already looked at. The rest of this chapter describes the United States in terms of its landscapes as we move east to west.

Coastal Plains

This enormous lowland region runs all the way down the Atlantic coast of the United States, from Cape Cod in Massachusetts to Florida and then across the gulf coast from Florida to the Rio Grande (meaning, of course, "Large River") in Texas.

If we look down from the air on the eastern part of this area, called the Atlantic Coastal Plain, we see that it features deepwater ports in bustling cities such as Boston. Continuing along the Atlantic coast, we find inlets and bays dotting the shoreline in Delaware and Virginia. Farther south, the Sea Islands form a chain off the Georgia coast. Marshes and swamps in the Florida Everglades mark the end of the Atlantic Coastal Plains.

The Gulf Coastal Plain runs inland farther than the Atlantic Coastal Plain. Much of the runoff water from the Gulf Coastal Plain drains into the mighty Mississippi River. Beginning as tiny streams that feed Lake Itasca in Minnesota and running 2,340 miles (3,765 kilometers), this longest U.S. river creates an expanding delta near the port city of New Orleans.

Appalachian Mountains

To the west of the Atlantic Coastal Plain lie the Appalachian Mountains. Not only are the Appalachian Mountains the second-longest mountain range in North America, they're also the oldest. Worn away over time by rain and wind, the Appalachian peaks have rounded tops. People who climb the highest peak, Mount Mitchell in North Carolina at 6,684 feet (2,037 meters), get a feel for how the mountains once hindered early settlers in their westward journey. Nowadays, the world's longest hiking trail snakes through these mountains. Completed in 1937, the Appalachian Trail passes through fourteen states, from Maine to Georgia.

Interior Plains

The Interior Plains blanket the center of the United States. The eastern part, called the Central Lowlands, boasts fields of spring wheat, river valleys layered with silt, thick forests, and grassy hills.

To the north of the Central Lowlands, the Great Lakes—five connected freshwater lakes—cover 95,000 square miles (246,000 square kilometers). Formed by glaciers, Lakes Superior, Michigan, Huron, Erie, and Ontario flow into the St. Lawrence River and form a major shipping route leading to the Atlantic Ocean.

To the west of the Central Lowlands lie the Great Plains, a broad, higher area, ranging from about 2,500 feet (762 meters) on its eastern edge to about 6,500 feet (981 meters) at its western end. Once famous for grazing American bison (buffalo), the Great Plains now feature fields of grain and cattle ranches. Beneath these rolling plains lie deposits of coal, oil, and natural gas.

Rocky Mountains

The largest mountain range in North America towers high above the Great Plains, with peaks reaching up to 14,000 feet (4,270 meters). The Rocky Mountains started forming 75 million years ago when the ocean floor rose in a giant arch. Wind, rain, and ice constantly shape the Rockies. The Continental Divide, an imaginary line along the mountains' peaks, separates streams flowing westward from those flowing eastward. Major rivers beginning in the Rockies include the Missouri and Rio Grande east of the divide and the Snake and Colorado to the west.

The Rockies challenged settlers traveling west, many of whom followed the South Pass in the Wyoming Basin. Modern-day travelers explore the many national parks in the Rocky Mountains, including Yellowstone, Glacier, and Grand Teton (TEE tahn). Hikers hope to glimpse the bighorn sheep, grizzly bear, Rocky Mountain goat, and mountain lion that roam these rugged peaks.

The Pacific

The Pacific Ocean is <u>flanked</u> on its east by the Sierra Nevada and Cascade mountain ranges. The Sierra Nevada has a dozen granite peaks rising more than fourteen thousand feet (forty-two hundred meters). Groves of giant sequoia, one of the world's tallest trees, grow here. Melting snow from the mountaintops irrigates orchards and grain fields in the California valleys below. Lake Tahoe, Nevada, nestles in the north face.

Where the Sierra Nevada ends, the Cascade Range begins. Named for the waterfalls of the Columbia River, which slices east to west through the middle of the range, the Cascades are volcanic rock. One peak, Mount St. Helens in Washington, violently erupted in 1980.

The Pacific region includes Hawaii and Alaska. Volcanoes rising up from the bottom of the Pacific Ocean form the Hawaiian Islands. Coral reefs border the oldest islands, in the west. The largest state in area, Alaska contains snowcapped mountains, glaciers, unspoiled forests, and volcanoes. The Pacific Mountain System hugs Alaska's south coast. In this rugged region, black, grizzly, Kodiak, and polar bears roam. Seals, walrus, and humpback and killer whales swim in Alaska's seas.

CHANGING REGIONS

Whole regions and parts of regions constantly undergo change. Alaska illustrates an area that changed as people discovered ways to use its natural resources. When Secretary of State William Seward arranged to purchase Alaska from the Russians for $7.2 million, his critics called the area Seward's Folly. Only about 33,000 Alaskans lived there back then. Then more than 30,000 people poured in during the gold rush of 1898. Today, the population has swelled to almost 627,000. Instead of gold, residents mine oil and gas at the reservoir near Prudhoe Bay. Alaska now provides products worth billions of dollars to the American economy.

Another area that underwent a dramatic change is the cotton belt in the Southeast. Before the Civil War, plantations powered by slave labor grew cotton on a large scale. After the war freed slaves and boll weevils invaded the cotton belt, the

Old South gradually transformed into the sun belt. Relying less on growing cotton and more on growing industry, the region attracted new residents. The sun belt's climate, combined with the invention of air-conditioning, has made this area popular with workers, retirees, and tourists.

! Implications

> To answer the question, "Why does all this matter?" or "What does it mean?," share the following insights with your child.

New economic ventures and changing populations have changed regions. This tendency started in the nineteenth century, when European settlers almost killed the vast herds of American bison that grazed on the Great Plains and gradually began to change the area into amber fields of grain and cattle ranches. After the Civil War, industrialization converted many regions from agriculture to manufacturing. Today the trend continues, with high-tech industries opening up across the states. In fact, some people have raised the interesting question of whether the regions of the United States are becoming too much the same.

The U.S. population continues to soar, growing more than 13 percent since 1990 to an estimated 281,400,000 in April 2000. This growth creates problems across the boundaries of many regions, including increasingly crowded cities and pollution and overuse of natural resources. At the dawn of the twenty-first century, new challenges lurk on the horizon for all the regions in the United States.

✓ *Fact Checker*

To check that your child knows or can find the basic facts in this chapter, have him or her fill in part of this chart (also called a graphic organizer). Your child can work, say, on two rows alone, and you can do two or more with his or her help.

FACTS ABOUT THE REGIONS

Region	Natural resource	Human-made landmark	Big city	Food product
New England				
Mid-Atlantic				
Southeast				
Midwest				
Southwest				
West				
Hawaii				
Alaska				

Answers appear in the back, preceding the index.

? The Big Questions

The following questions encourage your child to think critically rather than simply recall facts. If necessary, review the specific information from the preceding pages that will help your child make the appropriate inferences to come up with reasonable answers.

1. What is the best thing and what is the worst thing about living in your region? In answering, you can comment on climate, sports, entertainment, schools, and so on.
2. If you could live in any other region of the United States, which would you choose? Explain your answer.

Answers

Both questions ask for observations and opinions in addition to hard facts. Accept any reasonable answers that your child is able to support with specifics.

Skills Practice

The following activities give your child practice in applying the skills basic to social studies. For some of the activities, your child may need to review the information in the preceding pages.

A. INTERVIEWING

Select for your child an interviewee who is an older friend or family member and has lived in your region for a long time. Then give your child the following instructions.

Speak with an older person about changes to your region. Have questions ready before you meet. Something the person says may make you ask a follow-up or brand-new question. Here are some starters.

1. Over the years, what changes have you seen to this region? Have new businesses replaced old ones? How has the population changed? What was it like growing up in this region?
2. Was this region more fun when you were young or for young people today? Explain.
3. Are you happy or sad that you stayed in this region? Why?

Take notes as the person talks, or ask if you can record the conversation. Then, based on the notes or tape, write a summary of the interview, and share it with friends, family, or classmates. Send a thank-you note to your interviewee.

Evaluating Your Child's Skills: To do this project successfully, your child needs to prepare and maybe rehearse. Consider acting as the interviewee in a dry run for practice. You might also model asking questions and listening to responses.

B. ADVERTISING

Suggest that your child create a flyer or brochure promoting things to do in and near your town or city. The audience for this piece of writing is children who have just moved from another town or region. Give the following instructions.

1. Ask yourself, "If you were moving here, what would you want to find out about the town or region?" Identify categories you want to emphasize—for example, sports, movies and other entertainment, shopping, schools, and day trips out of town.
2. For each category, brainstorm the most important points to make. Then write a first draft "advertising" these activities or places. Get

reactions from readers, and then revise as necessary.

3. Find pictures from local publications, take photographs, or draw pictures to go with your writing.

4. Arrange your words and pictures in an attractive way, and make up a title or headline for your flyer or brochure.

> **Evaluating Your Child's Skills:** **To do this project successfully, your child needs to think of things he or she likes to do. Once your child has a list, help by suggesting strong verbs and colorful adjectives to describe activities and places.**

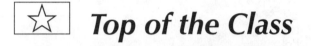

☆ Top of the Class

> **Following is a language arts activity that children can do on their own or share in class to show that they have been seriously considering the topic of U.S. regions.**

READING POETRY ALOUD

Find and read a poem about one of the regions in the United States. Read the poem through to yourself several times. Then practice reading the poem aloud—slowly and clearly so that your audience will understand and appreciate what you and the poet are saying.

One book you may want to look for in the library is *My America,* edited by Lee Bennett Hopkins (Simon & Schuster, 2000). It includes maps, statistics, other facts, and poems about all regions of the United States. Here are some individual poems to look for at home, at school, in the public library, or on the Internet.

Rosemary and Stephen Vincent Benét, "Western Wagons" [Midwest and West]

Sandra Cisneros, "Twister Hits Houston" [Southwest]

Emily Dickinson, "I'll Tell You How the Sun Rose" [New England]

Robert Frost, "Dust of Snow" or "The Runaway" or "A Hillside Thaw" [New England]

Nikki Giovanni, "Knoxville, Tennessee" [Southeast]

Langston Hughes, "Juke Box Love Song" [Mid-Atlantic]

Vachel Lindsay, "An Indian Summer Day on the Prairie" or "The Flower-Fed Buffaloes" [Midwest]

Claude McKay, "Spring in New Hampshire" [New England]

N. Scott Momaday, "To a Child Running with Outstretched Arms in Canyon de Chelly" [Southwest]

Pat Mora, "Mi Madre" [Southwest]

Carl Sandburg, "Chicago" [Midwest]

Walt Whitman, "City of Ships" [Mid-Atlantic]

CHAPTER 7
Geography of the World by Continent

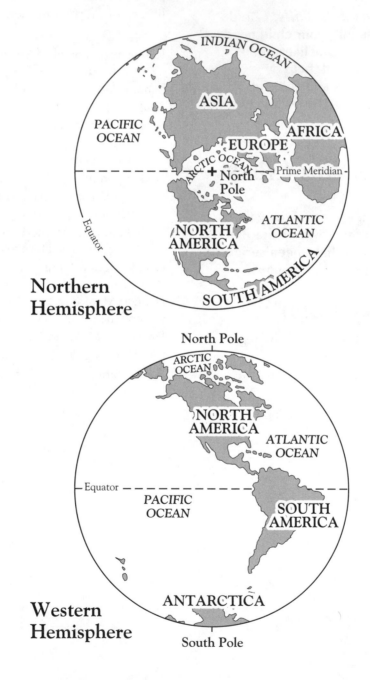

Four hemispheres of Earth

A continent is a continuous land mass. From largest to smallest, the continents are Asia, Africa, North America, South America, Antarctica, Europe, and Australia. These illustrations of the four hemispheres show different parts of continents. The following pages examine the seven continents. They provide and comment on important facts about each continent. Maps of the world and its continents appear in Appendix C.

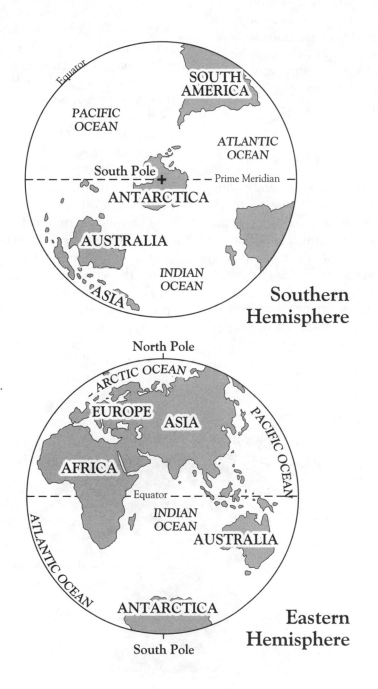

Southern Hemisphere

Eastern Hemisphere

What Your Child Needs to Know

You may choose to use the following text in several different ways, depending on your child's strengths and preferences. You might read the passage aloud; you might read it to yourself and then paraphrase it for your child; or you might ask your child to read the material along with you or on his or her own. *Remember to refer to the maps in the appendix.*

INTRODUCTION TO CONTINENTS

Astronauts blasting off into outer space and looking back down at Earth spot a planet of blue oceans divided by seven large masses of land called continents. These continents make up almost 30 percent of Earth's surface, an area of about 57 million square miles (148 million square kilometers).

Many millions of years ago, this scene appeared completely different. Earth contained a single huge continent called Pangaea. Sections of this supercontinent slowly broke up to create the seven continents of today.

Millions of years into the future, this arrangement may change again. Since pieces of Earth's crust (see Chapter 3) are constantly in motion, its continents may bump into each other or drift apart.

Some continents have similar features, but each continent has its own special features. For example, certain plants and animals may show up on every continent, but other plants and animals may belong on only one continent. In either case, every living thing and all the natural resources on each continent link to one another, and one small change might somersault into a chain reaction.

Let's explore all seven land masses and discover their attractions. Some of the countries described, such as Indonesia and the Philippines, are actually islands or groups of islands, not physically part of a land mass. Nevertheless, these islands are generally considered part of a nearby continent because of their similar culture, politics, language, history, economy, or other characteristics.

The following chart functions as a preview of each continent by listing the countries that make up the continent and providing some statistics about the continent. The text that follows the chart does not discuss every country on each continent. For specific information on each country, see Appendix B. The continents appear on the chart and in the following pages in order from largest to smallest.

240 MILLION YEARS AGO

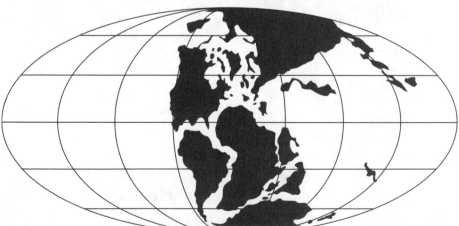

Earth as its continents appeared 240 million years ago

CONTINENTS AND THEIR COUNTRIES

ASIA

Area	Population	Highest point above sea level	Lowest point below sea level
55 million sq km (17 million sq mi)	3.6 billion	Mount Everest: 8,848 m (29,028 ft)	Dead Sea: −400 m (−1,312 ft)

Countries

Afghanistan	India	Malaysia	Sri Lanka
Armenia	Indonesia	Maldives	Syria
Azerbaijan	Iran	Mongolia	Taiwan
Bahrain	Iraq	Myanmar	Tajikistan
Bangladesh	Israel	Nepal	Thailand
Bhutan	Japan	Oman	Turkey
Brunei Darussalam	Jordan	Pakistan	Turkmenistan
Cambodia	Kazakhstan	Philippines	United Arab Emirates
China	Kuwait	Qatar	Uzbekistan
Cyprus	Kyrgyzstan	Republic of Korea	Vietnam
Democratic People's	Lao People's	(South Korea)	Yemen
Republic of Korea	Democratic Republic	Saudi Arabia	
(North Korea)	Lebanon	Singapore	

AFRICA

Area	Population	Highest point above sea level	Lowest point below sea level
30 million sq km (12 million sq mi)	770 million	Mount Kilimanjaro: 5,895 m (19,240 ft)	Lake Assal: −156 m (−512 ft)

Countries

Algeria	Djibouti	Malawi	Sierra Leone
Angola	Egypt	Mali	Somalia
Benin	Equatorial Guinea	Mauritania	South Africa
Botswana	Ethiopia	Mauritius	Sudan
Burkina Faso	Gabon	Morocco	Swaziland
Burundi	Gambia	Mozambique	Tanzania
Cameroon	Ghana	Namibia	Togo
Cape Verde	Guinea	Niger	Tunisia
Central African Republic	Guinea-Bissau	Nigeria	Uganda
Chad	Kenya	Rwanda	Zaire
Comoros	Lesotho	São Tomé and	Zambia
Congo, Republic of	Liberia	Príncipe	Zimbabwe
Côte d'Ivoire	Libya	Senegal	
(Ivory Coast)	Madagascar	Seychelles	

CONTINENTS AND THEIR COUNTRIES (Continued)

NORTH AMERICA

Area	Population	Highest point above sea level	Lowest point below sea level
24 million sq km (9 million sq mi)	481 million (including Puerto Rico; excluding Greenland)	Mount McKinley (Denali): 6,194 m (20,320 ft)	Death Valley: −86 m (−282 ft)

Countries

Antigua and Barbuda	Dominica	Honduras	St. Lucia
Bahamas	Dominican Republic	Jamaica	St. Vincent and the
Barbados	El Salvador	Mexico	Grenadines
Belize	Grenada	Nicaragua	Trinidad and Tobago
Canada	Guatemala	Panama	United States of
Cuba	Haiti	St. Kitts and Nevis	America

SOUTH AMERICA

Area	Population	Highest point above sea level	Lowest point below sea level
18 million sq km (7 million sq mi)	305 million	Aconcagua, Andes: 6,960 m (22,834 ft)	On Valdés Peninsula: −40 m (−131 ft)

Countries

Argentina	Chile	Guyana	Suriname
Bolivia	Colombia	Paraguay	Uruguay
Brazil	Ecuador	Peru	Venezuela

ANTARCTICA

Area	Population	Highest point above sea level	Lowest point below sea level
13 million sq km (5 million sq mi)	No permanent residents	Vinson Massif, Ellsworth Mountains: 4,897 m (16,066 ft)	Bedrock below Marie Byrd Land: −2,538 m (−8,327 ft)

CONTINENTS AND THEIR COUNTRIES (Continued)

EUROPE

Area	Population	Highest point above sea level	Lowest point below sea level
11 million sq km (4 million sq mi)	730 million	Mount Elbrus, Caucasus Mountains: 5,642 m (18,510 ft)	In the Caspian Sea: −28 m (−92 ft)

Countries

Albania	Finland	Lithuania	San Marino
Andorra	France	Luxembourg	Slovakia
Austria	Georgia	Macedonia	Slovenia
Belarus	Germany	Malta	Spain
Belgium	Greece	Moldova	Sweden
Bosnia and Herzegovina	Hungary	Netherlands	Switzerland
Bulgaria	Iceland	Norway	Ukraine
Croatia	Ireland	Poland	United Kingdom
Czech Republic	Italy	Portugal	Vatican City
Denmark	Latvia	Romania	Yugoslavia
Estonia	Liechtenstein	Russia	

AUSTRALIA (AND NEIGHBORS)

Area	Population	Highest point above sea level	Lowest point below sea level
8 million sq km (3 million sq mi)	18.7 million	Mount Kosciusko: 2,228 m (7,310 ft)	Lake Eyre: −16 m (−52 ft)

Countries

Australia	Kiribati	Papua New Guinea	Tuvalu
Federated States of Micronesia	Marshall Islands	Samoa	Vanuatu
	Nauru	Solomon Islands	
Fiji	New Zealand	Tonga	

Area and population figures from the textbook *Geography: The World and Its People* (Glencoe/McGraw-Hill, 2000) have been rounded. Highest point and lowest point data are from *Exploring Your World: The Adventure of Geography,* (National Geographic Society, 1993). Note that for Antarctica the figure for lowest point is for the lowest *known* point. This list does not include countries that are the possessions of other countries—for example, Greenland (possession of Denmark), New Caledonia (possession of France).

ASIA

The largest continent, containing nearly a third of Earth's land, is Asia. It ranges from China in the north to the Indonesian islands in the south, from the Philippines in the east to sections of Turkey and Russia in the west. Within its far-apart borders, which contain about 17 million square miles (44 million square kilometers), lie scorching deserts, freezing mountains, river valleys, plains and plateaus, and coasts fringing two oceans and many seas. More mountains rise up from Asia than from any other continent, including the world's highest—Mount Everest, peaking at just over 29,000 feet (8,800 meters) in the Himalayan range. Among Asia's countries are about half a dozen or so with names that end in *stan*, which means "land."

South Asia

The Himalayas create the northern border of India, in South Asia. This mountain range extends over about 229,500 square miles (594,400 square kilometers), primarily in India, but China and Pakistan also occupy portions. Ice constantly covers the mountaintops, but the lower slopes are green with pastures.

The Ganges (GAN jeez) River flows down the Himalayas to the Bay of Bengal. On its journey it provides water for the Ganges Plain, where crops such as tea, rice, and wheat grow. While the monsoon rains also water crops, they miss the parched Thar (TAHR) Desert (also called the Great Indian Desert), stretching along the border between India and Pakistan.

Several sandy deserts dot Pakistan. But all is not dry in this country, as five branches of the Indus River create rich river valleys for growing chickpeas, wheat, rice, and other crops. To the north stands the second-highest mountain in the world, K2, or Mount Godwin Austen. Passes through this mountain were once the primary way for people from the north to enter South Asia.

East Asia

China spreads across eastern Asia. In this third-largest country in the world, most of the land is either mountains or desert. Mountains surround the sand dunes of the Taklimakan (*tah* kluh muh KAN) Desert and the Plateau of Tibet—the world's biggest

plateau. The Chang, Huang (HWANG), and Xi (SHEE) river systems keep the eastern half of China well watered so that the main food crop—rice—can grow in paddies.

Japan is nicknamed Land of the Rising Sun because of its position in Earth's eastern region, where it is the first part of the globe to get the sun's light each day. This country forms an archipelago. Its islands are part of the Ring of Fire, a region plagued by earthquakes and volcanoes. Many of Japan's highest mountains—including the tallest, Mount Fuji—are volcanoes. Surrounded by the Sea of Japan to the west and the North Pacific Ocean to the east, Japan boasts a leading fishing industry.

Across the Sea of Japan lies the Korean Peninsula. The bottom region, South Korea, contains a coastline with many harbors for its fishing fleets. Above, North Korea's mountains and hills offer narrow valleys and plains for farmland where rice and vegetables grow.

Southeast Asia

The Southeast Asia region sweeps from eastern India to southern China. The peninsulas and tens of thousands of islands that make up the area span the equator. In this tropical environment with land rich in volcanic soil grow exotic fruits such as mangos and papayas. More volcanoes exist on the 13,677 islands of Indonesia than in any other country in the world. Below the rich soil lies a wealth of tin and copper, oil, and rubies and sapphires. Teak, ebony, and other tropical hardwoods grow in the rain forests.

Southwest Asia

This area runs from the Hindu Kush mountains in the east to the Sinai Peninsula in the west. Deserts in this part of Asia owe themselves to mountains and prevailing winds. The bodies of water bordering the region include the Mediterranean Sea, the Black and Caspian seas, the Persian Gulf, and the Arabian Sea. Many countries in Southwest Asia depend on oil exports for their economies.

Thousands of years ago, the people living in Southwest Asia were among the earliest in the world to farm and domesticate animals. Some of the world's oldest civilizations started and grew in the valley between the Tigris and Euphrates (yoo

FRAY teez) rivers. Judaism, Christianity, and Islam all began in Southwest Asia.

Many Names

Historians use the terms *Fertile Crescent, Mesopotamia, Holy Land,* and *Palestine* when discussing early human times in Southwest Asia. Politicians talk about *Arab nations* and the *Middle East* when discussing many of the countries in Southwest Asia. The last term also includes Egypt and Libya, which are on the continent Africa (see next section).

AFRICA

Africa is the second-largest continent and the only one to have a chunk of land in each of the four hemispheres. The equator slices through Africa. The world's longest river, the Nile, journeys 4,160 miles (6,695 kilometers) northward through Africa before pouring into the Mediterranean Sea. However, falls and rapids make the Nile difficult to navigate. While Africa contains the world's largest hot desert—the Sahara, which was once grassland—snow also appears on the continent, at the peak of its highest mountain—Mount Kilimanjaro. (Reports in 2001 of melting snow there worried watchers of global warming.)

The Sahara and North Africa

Stretching out to an expanse almost as large as the United States, the Sahara covers around 3.5 million square miles (9 million square kilometers). The desert blankets most of North Africa, stretching westward from Egypt to the Atlantic Ocean. Here, water is scarce; sometimes years pass without rain. In Egypt, dry sand dunes contrast with the green Nile River valley. Sometimes the Nile floods, creating new, rich soil for crops such as cotton.

Many of these crops are exported through the Suez Canal, a waterway offering a shortcut to Asia. In Libya, to Egypt's west, oil from wells in the Sahara travel through huge pipelines to storage tanks and then overseas. (Note that geographers consider eastern Egypt—the Sinai Peninsula—part of Southwest Asia, not Africa.)

West Africa

In West Africa, the countries nearest the Sahara are themselves deserts or desertlike. These countries form a group called the Sahel; the name *Sahel* means "border."

Farther south of the Sahara, large plateaus resembling a series of grassy steps cover much of the land. Here, crops such as cacao, used to make chocolate, and peanuts grow. Farmers also harvest tropical crops including cassava, a plant root used to make bread flour.

Along West Africa's Atlantic coastline lie tropical rain forests and swamps. The Niger River stretches 2,590 miles (4,168 kilometers) through the western section of Africa, flowing into the Gulf of Guinea off Nigeria. The country of Nigeria is Africa's most populous nation and also Africa's leading producer of crude oil, a liquid raw material that yields petroleum.

Central Africa

When people picture Africa, many imagine the steamy tropical rain forests and grasslands of the Republic of the Congo in Central Africa. Here, tangles of trees and vines form a canopy, blocking out sunlight from the rain forest floor. Monkeys nibbling food swing through the canopy while parrots chatter. Workers harvest tropical woods from the rain forests.

The powerful Congo River snakes 2,900 miles (4,505 kilometers) through the forests before tumbling into the Atlantic Ocean. To the north and south of the river, zebras, giraffes, lions, and other wildlife graze on grasslands. Natural resources in this region include copper, cobalt, and diamonds.

East Africa

East Africa borders the Red Sea and the Indian Ocean. Along the coastline, palm trees sway on white beaches. Below the equator, Tanzania (*tan* zuh NEE uh) incorporates a chunk of the Great Rift Valley, created when two plates making up Earth's crust moved apart long ago. At that time, lava flowed out of these **rifts,** or openings, to form Mount Kilimanjaro, which rises 19,340 feet (5,895 meters) above Tanzania's plains.

This country also contains Africa's largest lake—Lake Victoria. Lions and antelopes visit the lake during dry season. Tourists visit the Serengeti National Park to photograph these creatures. In neighboring Kenya, visitors take photo safaris through parks built on vast plains. Many species of endangered wildlife roam freely, safe from illegal hunting, and attracting the country's main source of income—tourists.

Southern Africa

The Republic of South Africa, at the tip of the continent, borders both the Atlantic and Indian oceans. For years, most attention paid to South Africa concerned the country's apartheid, or racial segregation, practices. The apartheid policy ended in 1991, and people in South Africa have been working toward greater democracy.

One of this country's natural wonders is diamonds. The Cullinan diamond, the world's largest, tipped the scales at more than three thousand carats. Today, miners cut through rock to locate diamonds, along with gold and copper. Farmers raise "black diamonds" of their own—karakul sheep nicknamed for their shiny black coats.

In the center of South Africa lies a high, grassy plateau that European settlers called a veld. There lions and cheetahs hunt antelope. In the cliffs called the Great Escarpment, which circle the veld, leopards prowl. (An **escarpment** is a steep cliff that divides high and low ground.)

In the vast Kalahari (*kah* luh HAR ee) Desert of Botswana (bat SWA nuh), about half the San people (formerly called bushmen) are nomads, as were their ancestors. They gather nuts and fruits, search for water, and kill animals such as leopards. The other half of the San have taken up a settled lifestyle; they mostly work on farms. To the north of the Kalahari, the Okavango (*oh* kuh VANG goh) Swamps cover a huge marshy area in Botswana.

The Zambezi (zam BEE zee) River forms the border between Botswana's neighbors, Zimbabwe (zim BAH bwee) and Zambia (ZAM bee uh). The river suddenly drops 355 feet (108 meters) in spectacular Victoria Falls. African people call the falls *Musi-oa-Tunya*, "the smoke that thunders."

Off the southeastern coast of Africa in the Indian Ocean lies the island of Madagascar (ma duh GAS kuhr). This country is the world's largest producer of vanilla beans. A monkeylike animal called the lemur makes its home in the trees of Madagas-

car. To the north lie the 110 islands of the Seychelles (say SHELZ). Giant tortoises live along the coasts of these islands, and sharks cruise the surrounding Indian Ocean.

NORTH AMERICA

North America, the third-largest continent, contains Canada, the United States, Mexico, the Central American countries, and the Caribbean archipelago, sometimes referred to as the West Indies. Greenland belongs to Denmark, a country in Europe, but counts, geographically, as part of North America.

Another way to describe North America is to say that the continent extends from a frozen polar north to the tropics. In between are snowcapped mountains, deserts, wheat-covered plains, rain forests, and the longest coastline of any continent. While North America is extremely narrow in Panama, up north the expanse of North America covers half the globe: it reaches from the Aleutian (uh LOO shuhn) Islands to Greenland.

Canada

Although the name *Canada* comes from an Iroquois (ihr ruh KWOI) word meaning "small village," it is actually the second-largest country in the world and contains the greatest number of lakes and waterways. Three oceans lap at Canada's shores: the Atlantic to the east, the Pacific to the west, and the Arctic to the north. North of the Arctic Circle lie many islands, the northernmost covered in glacial ice. Farther south, lakes shaped by glaciers and ancient rocks dot the still-frozen Canadian Shield.

People who venture here generally have only bear, moose, and reindeer for neighbors. To the east, the Appalachian Highlands give rise to a mountain range that knows no border but, instead, continues right down the eastern United States. To the west, the Rocky Mountains and Coast Mountains also cross the Canada–United States border into the United States and continue south. Likewise, Canada's central Interior Plains, with its rich soil, extend southward and become the Great Plains of the United States. The two countries share the Great Lakes and the awesome Niagara Falls, at the point where Lake Erie tumbles into Lake Ontario.

The United States

To Canada's south, the United States is the fourth-largest country in the world. Its landscape shifts from region to region (see Chapter 6 for two ways of thinking about U.S. regions). In the east, the Appalachians wend all the way down to Alabama, and in the west, the Rockies make their way down to Mexico. Smack in the center of the country, the Great Plains offer the perfect environment for growing corn, wheat, and other grains. Rivers crisscross the United States. The mighty Mississippi is probably the most famous. It runs from Minnesota to Louisiana, draining most of the Gulf Coastal Plain, which borders the Gulf of Mexico.

A national park system protects wildlife and fantastic geographic features of the United States. A sample of the parks includes Yellowstone (in Wyoming, Idaho, and Montana), where visitors await the eruption of Old Faithful—a **geyser** that spurts hot water into the air; the Everglades (in Florida), where panthers hide in cypress swamps; and Sequoia National Park (in California), where enormous redwood trees, including the world's largest, tower above the forest floor.

Mexico

South of the United States, Mexico earned the nickname "land of the shaking earth" because the land shook the civilizations that first lived there. Mexico City continues to shake occasionally with earthquakes and volcanoes.

A peninsula juts out from each side of Mexico: Baja (BAH hah) California into the Pacific Ocean and the Yucatán (*yoo* kuh TAN) Peninsula into the Gulf of Mexico. (The Yucatán Peninsula also includes parts of Central America, discussed next.) The Rio Grande forms a natural boundary between parts of Mexico and the United States. It empties into the gulf. Three mountain ranges shape Mexico's landscape: south of Mexico City, the Sierra Madre del Sur; along the western coast, the Sierra Madre Occidental; and along the eastern coast, the Sierra Madre Oriental. In between, lie the plains and deserts of the Plateau of Mexico.

Oil, minerals, and metals such as silver exist in this rugged land. Although Mexico's mountain and desert regions don't support crops, avocados, bananas, sugarcane, and other foods do grow in parts of the country, and the cocao trees of the jungle produce pods for chocolate.

Central America and the West Indies

Southeast of Mexico lies Central America. This one-thousand-mile (sixteen-hundred-kilometer) land bridge to South America has the Pacific Ocean on its west coast and the Caribbean Sea, part of the Atlantic Ocean, on its east coast. Given that the land is very narrow in spots, engineers were able to construct the Panama Canal, a fifty-one-mile (eighty-two-kilometer) passage from the Atlantic to the Pacific. Ships no longer have to travel all the way down one side of South America and up the other side to carry cargo from, say, New Orleans to Los Angeles.

Mountain ranges rise in the seven countries that make up Central America, and volcanoes are a threat to life and the economy. The area's rich soil, though, yields bananas, coffee, and sugarcane. In addition, researchers create new medicines from rare plants growing in the tropical rain forests.

All the Central American countries except Belize (buh LEEZ) share a mostly North American and Spanish cultural heritage. Belize, once ruled by the British, has strong British and African influences.

Off the east coast, mountains rising out of the Caribbean Sea shape the West Indies. The Caribbean cultures mingle African, North American, European, and Asian styles.

This chain of islands extends in a southeast curve from the Bahamas to Trinidad and Tobago. Seasonal hurricanes slap their tropical beaches. On the larger islands of Cuba and Puerto Rico, sugarcane, coffee, and other tropical crops grow in the lush central highlands. Perhaps the most important natural resource, however, is the sun, cherished by tourists visiting during the winter months.

SOUTH AMERICA

The fourth-largest continent, South America ranges from the southern border of tropical Panama in Central America to the Tierra del Fuego (foo AY goh) islands near frosty Antarctica. It is a continent with significant waterways, mountains, and plant and animal life.

The Andes (AN deez) rise out of the Caribbean Sea in the north to begin the world's longest mountain chain on land—about 4,000 miles (6,437 kilometers). The mountains reach into Venezuela, Colombia, Ecuador, Peru, Bolivia, and Argentina. Within the Argentina Andes stands the highest peak in the Western Hemisphere, Mount Aconcagua (ah kuhn KAH gwuh), rising almost 23,000 feet (7,000 meters).

High up in the Andes Mountains of Peru begins the Amazon River, the world's largest in volume, with more than a thousand branches. Early explorers called the river "Sweet Water Sea" because at the point where its powerful waters pour into the Atlantic, it pushes back the saltwater for nearly 100 miles (161 kilometers). Rather than tasting salty, the seawater in this zone tastes fresh. The river flows through an enormous tropical rain forest covering one-third of the continent.

Within South America's borders are Lake Titicaca (ti ti KAH kuh), the highest large lake in the world, and La Paz (PAHZ), the highest large city in the world. And the world's highest waterfall, Angel Falls, drops more than 3,200 feet (975 meters) from Devil Mountain in Venezuela.

Spreading out over almost half of South America, Brazil boasts the longest coastline of any country in the world. The beaches of Rio de Janeiro (REE oh day zhuh NEHR oh), Brazil, on the tropic of Capricorn, fringe the Atlantic Ocean. In the north and west of Brazil, the Amazon River basin contains an amazing variety of plants. Brazil nuts grow in tall trees, and in the rain forests enormous trees taller than twenty-story buildings block out the sun. About one in ten of Earth's plants and animals lives in this environment.

Domesticated animals roam Argentina's pampas, grasslands that cover most of the southern region of South America. Here, cowboys called gauchos tend sheep and cattle on huge ranches. Seemingly endless rows of corn and fields of wheat, along with the vast pasturelands, cover the pampas.

Other animals thrive high up in the Andes. In these rocky, snow-covered peaks, people raise llamas and their close cousins, guanacos, as pack animals and for their fur. At the tip of Argentina, lies the world's southernmost town—Ushuaia (oo SWEE uh), in Tierra del Fuego—where most of the islanders raise sheep.

Among South America's exports are bananas, coffee, petroleum, textiles, tin, and copper.

Out in the South Pacific Ocean about twenty-three hundred miles (thirty-seven hundred kilometers) west of Chile, lies Easter Island, famous for more than six hundred huge statues. Carved from single blocks of stone, they are thought to be monuments created by competing clans of islanders.

> ### Another Name
>
> *Latin America* is an umbrella name for Mexico, Central America, the West Indies, and South America.

ANTARCTICA

A gigantic sheet of ice blankets nearly 98 percent of Antarctica, the fifth-largest continent. This is the coldest, windiest, highest, and driest continent in the world. Although this region contains 70 percent of the world's freshwater, all is frozen in a polar ice cap up to 2 miles (3.2 kilometers) thick. Situated around the South Pole, which is Earth's southernmost point, and surrounded by frozen oceans, Antarctica can reach temperatures of −100° F (−73° C). Three months out of the year, this continent experiences total darkness; for another three months, the sun never sets.

Researchers from around the world populate Antarctica. There are no native people, and no countries own the land. At McMurdo Station on Ross Island, American scientists study the environment and wildlife. Only a few species can survive on the 5 million square miles (13 million square kilometers) of this icy continent. Ice algae and mosses grow along the coast. A few insects exist on land. In Antarctica's waters, colorless icefish, whales, and seals eat krill—small, shrimplike shellfish. In rocky rookeries, or breeding places, male emperor penguins hatch eggs.

Scientists discovered fossils, or remains of ancient plants and animals, that paint a different picture of Antarctica millions of years ago. Dinosaurs and small mammals once wandered the land, which was much warmer and covered with green forests and plants. Scientists have noted that in recent years more of Antarctica is melting than usual. They wonder what this change will mean.

Beneath the ice, scientists have discovered mountains, valleys, and huge lakes. Scientists also believe that this continent contains a fortune in minerals and petroleum hidden under the ice and offshore. Mining these riches has been put on permanent hold because of Antarctica's fragile environment.

EUROPE

Although the second-smallest continent, with only 7 percent of Earth's land, Europe contains more than forty countries and a population more than twice that of South America. Europe and Asia are parts of the world's most enormous land mass, referred to by some as Eurasia. However, geographers consider Europe one continent and Asia another because of cultural differences. In this view, the Ural (YOOR uhl) Mountains of Russia separate Europe from Asia.

Most European countries are close to one or more large bodies of water—the Arctic and Atlantic oceans and the Caspian, Mediterranean, Black, and other seas. The network of rivers that crisscrosses Europe easily links ports with major cities.

Other important mountain chains of Europe include the Pyrenees, which divide France and Spain, and the Alps (the continent's highest mountain range), which extend over the southern and central regions. At the base of the mountains, rolling plains provide productive farmland.

The British Isles

The British Isles stand slightly apart from the mainland of Europe but are part of Europe. They consist of the Republic of Ireland and the United Kingdom (the latter includes England, Scotland, Wales, and Northern Ireland). Lush meadows that remain green because of a damp climate earned Ireland its nickname—Emerald Isle. The fertile Lowlands of Scotland contrast with towering Highlands sliced by **lochs** (lakes). Farther south, in England, is a patchwork of green fields, mountains, forests, **moors** (open land, often marshy), and wide beaches. Offshore, workers mine oil and gas from under the North Sea and harvest fish such as salmon.

Northern Europe

The area known as Scandinavia extends from the Arctic Ocean to the North Sea and consists of the countries Denmark, Norway, Sweden, Iceland, and Finland. In its most northern reaches, Scandinavia is famous as "the land of the midnight sun," where the sun shines twenty-four hours a day in the summertime.

Movement of glaciers caused **fjords** (long, narrow ocean inlets with steep walls) along Norway's coastline, and these fjords create excellent fishing ports. Just east of Norway, Finland harvests its enormous forests for wood and paper products. To the south, part of Denmark is on the Jutland Peninsula. Denmark once ruled the islands of Greenland and Iceland. Today, despite its historical and political background, Greenland counts as part of North America. The rugged island of Iceland rests below the Arctic Circle. Some Icelanders get their heat from geysers and harness their electricity from the power of melting glaciers. Since three-quarters of the land is barren, they make their living from fishing.

Northwestern Europe

Much of Europe's northwestern region contains mountain ranges. For example, the world-famous Swiss Alps run across Switzerland and Austria. Here the much photographed Matterhorn rises 14,691 feet (4,478 meters), and rivers such as the Rhine begin. The Rhine and the Bavarian Alps travel through Germany. Once covered with thick woods such as the Black Forest, Germany today has a varied landscape of plains, mountain meadows, and shallow lakes. Within northwestern Europe, the fertile North European Plain contains rich soil for growing grains, vegetables, and fruits, including grapes for wine.

Southern Europe

The Pyrenees divide France of northwestern Europe from the Iberian Peninsula of southern Europe. Spain occupies most of the peninsula. In the interior, a high and dry plateau covers almost half of the country. Sandy beaches along the Mediterranean coast attract tourists. At the southern tip of Spain, the Strait of Gibraltar divides Europe from Africa.

To the east, mountains and hills form three-quarters of Italy. The rocks supply stone, such as marble, and salt. Italy's tallest volcano—Mount Etna at 11,122 feet (3,390 meters)—still erupts. On lower slopes throughout Italy, olives, nuts, and grapes grow.

Greece, east of Italy, is mainly mountains, and its nearly two thousand islands are tops of mountains. On the Greek mainland, the Pindus Mountains run down the center. Fertile valleys and plains, where lemons and olives grow, cut through the mountains.

Eastern Europe

In contrast, few mountains rise from the rolling land of eastern Europe. The North European Plain rolls across Poland, with the lowlands rising into the Carpathian (kar PAY thee uhn) Mountains at the country's southern border. The Vistula (VIS chuh luh) River winds through Poland and provides water for crops such as sugar beets and potatoes. Another river, the Danube (DAN yoob), twists through Hungary, separating its capital into two cities: Buda and Pest.

The enormous republic of Russia covers 6.6 million square miles (17.1 million square kilometers) and straddles two continents—Europe and Asia. Befitting the world's largest country, Russia accommodates incredible geographic variety. A gigantic plain, grassy in the south and forested in the north, covers much of the land. The Ural Mountains split the Northern European Plain in the European section from the West Siberian Plain in the Asian section. Farther east lies the Central Siberian Plateau, followed by the Eastern Siberian Uplands. In the far north, hills covered year-round with ice and frozen earth rim the cold Arctic Ocean. Within Russia's boundaries is the tallest mountain on the European continent—Mount Elbrus (EL broos), rising 18,510 feet (5,642 meters); the deepest lake on Earth—Lake Baikal (beye KAL); and the world's largest lake—the Caspian Sea.

AUSTRALIA

Australia is both the smallest continent and the biggest island. This island continent sometimes goes by the nickname "Land Down Under" because of its location in the Southern Hemisphere.

The flat land of Australia appears red in many places because the soil contains rusty-colored iron oxide.

Australia is also very dry; more than two-thirds of the continent is desert or wild bush. Some areas have no rainfall for years at a time. **Billabongs,** or "dead rivers," contain water for a portion of the year. They flood during the wet season, from November to April, but during the dry season, from May to October, the hot desert heat dries up every drop. Because so much of Australia's land is arid, most of the people live along the more fertile coasts. One area not so parched is the Great Barrier Reef, a chain of five hundred islands and coral reefs off Australia's northeastern coast. The skeletons of tiny sea creatures called coral polyps formed the reef, which stretches 1,250 miles (2,011 kilometers) in the Pacific waters. Colorful fish swim alongside sharks and poisonous lionfish.

Creatures that live only in Australia include **marsupials,** mammals that carry their young in a pouch. Examples include the kangaroo, wallaby, koala, and wombat. A flightless bird called an emu zips across the open grassland. The platypus, a furry swimming mammal with a duck bill and webbed feet, lays eggs and makes milk for its young after they hatch. Dingoes, or wild dogs, wander the outback, the sparsely settled inland areas. On fertile plains and in the Murray River Valley, Merino sheep and lambs graze.

Neighbors

Two nearby neighbors of Australia are two "non-continents": the country of New Zealand and the Pacific Island region known as Oceania (*oh* shee AH nee uh). About 1,200 miles (1,930 kilometers) southeast of Australia, New Zealand consists of two main islands and many tinier ones. Mountains, fertile green land, and fjords contrast with Australia's deserts.

The approximately twenty-five thousand islands that make up Oceania contain different landscapes. Tropical rain forests and rugged mountains cover some. Volcanoes or coral reefs formed others. Many of the islands, such as Tahiti, resemble a tropical postcard with swaying palm trees, lush mountains, and a turquoise lagoon.

! Implications

To answer the question, "Why does all this matter?" or "What does it mean?," share the following insights with your child.

- Many questions, and even controversy, arise when classifying land masses as continents. For example, after Christopher Columbus and his followers made voyages to the New World, people on the continents of Europe, Asia, and Africa counted North America and South America as two continents. In 1801, they added Australia to the list of continents and then Antarctica in 1820. But since some people believe that Europe is a peninsula of Asia and refer to the combined continent as Eurasia, then perhaps North America and South America, linked by Central America, should count as only a single continent.

- Some regions and countries straddle two continents. The Middle East is partially in Africa and partially in Asia; Russia is in both Europe and Asia.

- Usually islands "go with" a continent that is close by or that has a cultural or political connection to it. For example, we say that the Philippine Islands are part of the continent Asia. However, even though Hawaii is a state of the United States, it is *not* part of the continent North America or any other continent. It's not even part of the region called Oceania. The Hawaiian Islands are simply "out there," by themselves.

- Earth's continents are constantly in motion, as if they were unanchored boats bobbing upon the sea. Scientists tell us that all seven continents are journeying in various directions. For example, North America and Europe are drifting farther apart, at the annual rate of around 1 inch (2.5 centimeters). Similarly, the gap between East Africa and the rest of Africa grows .04 inch (.1 centimeter) wider each year. These measurements may not seem like much on a yearly basis, but the land areas may continue to drift for a long, long time and may transform Earth as we know it.

✓ Fact Checker

To check that your child knows or can find the basic facts in this chapter, here are questions about some of its major points. Your child should circle his or her answer—*T* for "true" or *F* for "false."

TRUE OR FALSE?

1. T F   The seven continents make up 70 percent of Earth's surface.
2. T F   Asia is the largest continent.
3. T F   The plants and animals of each continent are unique to that continent; they do not appear on any other continent.
4. T F   Each continent except Antarctica is partially on the equator.
5. T F   The world's highest waterfall, Angel Falls, is in South America.
6. T F   The Suez Canal connects the Atlantic and Pacific oceans.
7. T F   Antarctica is the smallest continent.
8. T F   A country cannot lie on more than one continent.
9. T F   An area in the Pacific is called the Ring of Fire because of its many earthquakes and volcanoes.
10. T F   Asia and Europe form a single enormous land mass.

Answers appear in the back, preceding the index.

? The Big Questions

The following questions encourage your child to think critically rather than simply recall facts. If necessary, review the specific information from the preceding pages that will help your child make the necessary inferences to come up with reasonable answers.

1. In addition to trade, why is it important for a country on one continent to have good relationships with countries on another continent?
2. Which continent would you most like to visit? Tell why.

Suggested Answers

1. *Your child may respond in terms of strategic alliances for military purposes. For example, after the World Trade Center tragedy in September 2001, the U.S. secretary of defense went to Pakistan and other countries to get support for actions the United States was planning to take against their neighbor, Afghanistan.*
2. *Your child's answer should give observations and opinions in addition to hard facts. Accept any reasonable answers that your child is able to support with specifics.*

Skills Practice

The following activities give your child practice in applying the skills basic to social studies. For some of the activities, your child may need to review the information in the preceding pages.

A. RESEARCHING CURRENT EVENTS: THE EUROPEAN UNION

Using a relatively recent encyclopedia, help your child learn the basic facts about the European Union, an organization with membership based on geography. Then by using a search engine for the Internet or by personally looking through print editions of recent newspapers and news magazines, your child can find more recent information.

Write a paragraph that answers one of the following questions about the European Union. Mention in the paragraph where you found the information that you provide.

1. What is the euro, and how are Europeans and people in the rest of the world responding to it these days?
2. On what recent issue have members of the European Union disagreed? What positions are different members taking on this issue?
3. On what recent issue have members of the European Union agreed? What action did the union take as a result?

Evaluating Your Child's Skills: In order to complete this activity successfully, your child needs to monitor his or her own reading comprehension. Once your child has found one or more comprehensible articles, he or she must prepare a paragraph, complete with a topic sentence and supporting details.

B. INTERPRETING A GRAPH

An important skill in social studies (as well as in most other subjects) is interpreting visuals—for example, bar graphs such as the one that follows.

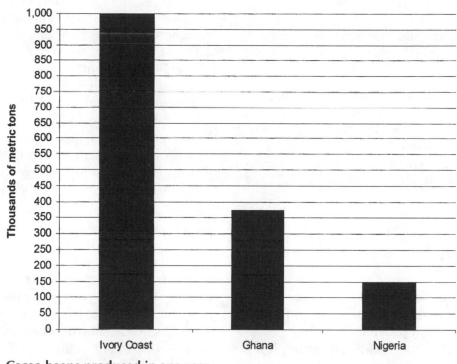

Cacao beans produced in one year

Examine the bar graph carefully, and answer the three questions about it.

1. Of the three West African countries represented on the bar graph, which one produced the most cacao beans in the year in question?
2. In total, how many tons of cocao beans did the three countries produce in one year?
3. How much more cacao did Ghana produce that year than Nigeria? Select your answer from the following choices.
   a. Five times as much
   b. More than twice as much
   c. Exactly twice as much

Answers

1. *Ivory Coast*
2. *Accept an answer of "around 1,525 metric tons" based on the following estimates of each bar: Ivory Coast, 1,000 metric tons; Ghana, about 375 metric tons; Nigeria, about 150 metric tons.*
3. *b*

Evaluating Your Child's Skills: **In order to answer the questions correctly, your child needs to understand what each bar means and needs to estimate the height of each bar. If he or she has trouble, draw a fourth bar for an imaginary country that produces 450,000 tons of cacao beans, and show your child how *you* read the fourth bar. At that point, your child will be able to articulate what each of the three original bars means.**

☆ *Top of the Class*

Children interested in delving more deeply into the topics covered in this chapter can choose one or more of the following activities. They may do the activities for their own satisfaction or report on what they have done to show that they have been seriously considering issues related to the continents.

A POINT TO PONDER

Suggest to your child that he or she raise the following issue in class.

Looking at the continents now, it appears that the east coast of South America and the west coast of Africa can fit together like the pieces of a jigsaw puzzle. Were South America and Africa joined at one point? How did scientists go about answering this question? What kinds of evidence did they look for?

VISITING SCHOOLS ON OTHER CONTINENTS

Introduce your child to the following Web site: www.ncsu.edu/midlink/cs/middle .home.html, which provides links to schools on other continents. For example, clicking on www.ais-dhaka.net takes users to a school in Bangladesh in Asia. Your child can bring up questions about virtual visits to schools—and his or her answers to them—in class.

1. Before you looked at this Web site, what did you expect of a school in Asia (or on any other continent)? How right or wrong were you?
2. What most surprised you about each school on another continent?
3. Based on Web sites, how is education on other continents similar to and different from the education you get?
4. In an e-mail exchange with someone in a school on another continent, what did you learn? And what did you say about yourself and your school?

READING POETRY

Find and read a poem (in English or in another language that you understand) about one of the countries in the world other than the United States. Read the poem through to yourself several times. Then practice reading the poem aloud—slowly and clearly so that your audience will understand and appreciate what you and the poet are saying.

Check your library for a recent book of poetry and art from many countries: *Voices*, edited by Barbara Brenner and published by the National Geographic Society in 2000.

APPENDIX A

States of the Union

State	Date of entry (order)	Capital	Area sq mi/sq km	Population (April 1, 2000)	Nickname	Region
Alabama	1819 (22)	Montgomery	52,237/135,293	4,447,100	Heart of Dixie	Southeast
Alaska	1959 (49)	Juneau	615,230/1,593,444	626,932	Last Frontier	Separate
Arizona	1912 (48)	Phoenix	114,006/295,276	5,130,632	Grand Canyon State	Southwest
Arkansas	1836 (25)	Little Rock	53,182/137,742	2,673,400	Land of Opportunity	Southeast
California	1850 (31)	Sacramento	158,869/411,470	33,871,648	Golden State	West
Colorado	1876 (38)	Denver	104,100/269,618	4,301,261	Centennial State	West
Connecticut	1788 (5)	Hartford	5,544/14,358	3,405,565	Constitution State	New England
Delaware	1787 (1)	Dover	2,396/6,206	783,600	First State	Mid-Atlantic
Florida	1845 (27)	Tallahassee	59,928/155,214	15,982,378	Sunshine State	Southeast
Georgia	1788 (4)	Atlanta	58,977/152,750	8,186,453	Empire State of the South; Goober State; Peach State	Southeast
Hawaii	1959 (50)	Honolulu	6,459/16,729	1,211,537	Aloha State	Separate
Idaho	1890 (43)	Boise	83,574/216,456	1,293,953	Gem State	West
Illinois	1818 (21)	Springfield	57,918/150,007	12,419,293	Prairie State	Midwest
Indiana	1816 (19)	Indianapolis	36,420/94,328	6,080,485	Hoosier State	Midwest
Iowa	1846 (29)	Des Moines	56,276/145,754	2,926,324	Hawkeye State	Midwest
Kansas	1861 (34)	Topeka	82,282/213,110	2,688,418	Sunflower State	Midwest
Kentucky	1792 (15)	Frankfort	40,411/104,665	4,041,769	Bluegrass State	Southeast
Louisiana	1812 (18)	Baton Rouge	49,651/128,595	4,468,976	Pelican State	Southeast
Maine	1820 (23)	Augusta	33,741/97,388	1,274,923	Pine Tree State	New England
Maryland	1788 (7)	Annapolis	12,297/31,849	5,296,486	Free State; Old Line State	Mid-Atlantic
Massachusetts	1788 (6)	Boston	9,241/23,934	6,349,097	Bay State	New England
Michigan	1837 (26)	Lansing	96,705/250,465	9,938,444	Wolverine State	Midwest
Minnesota	1858 (32)	St. Paul	86,943/225,182	4,919,479	North Star State	Midwest
Mississippi	1817 (20)	Jackson	48,286/125,060	2,844,658	Magnolia State	Southeast
Missouri	1821 (24)	Jefferson City	69,709/180,546	5,595,211	Show Me State	Midwest

State	Date of entry (order)	Capital	Area sq mi/sq km	Population (April 1, 2000)	Nickname	Region
Montana	1889 (41)	Helena	147,046/380,849	902,195	Treasure State	West
Nebraska	1867 (37)	Lincoln	77,358/200,358	1,711,263	Cornhusker State	Midwest
Nevada	1864 (36)	Carson City	110,567/286,367	1,998,257	Silver State	West
New Hampshire	1788 (9)	Concord	9,283/24,044	1,235,786	Granite State	New England
New Jersey	1787 (3)	Trenton	8,215/21,277	8,414,350	Garden State	Mid-Atlantic
New Mexico	1912 (47)	Santa Fe	121,598/314,939	1,819,046	Land of Enchantment	Southwest
New York	1788 (11)	Albany	53,989/139,833	18,976,457	Empire State	Mid-Atlantic
North Carolina	1789 (12)	Raleigh	52,672/136,421	8,049,313	Tar Heel State	Southeast
North Dakota	1889 (39)	Bismarck	70,704/183,123	642,200	Peace Garden State; Flickertail State	Midwest
Ohio	1803 (17)	Columbus	44,828/116,103	11,353,140	Buckeye State	Midwest
Oklahoma	1907 (46)	Oklahoma City	69,903/181,048	3,450,654	Sooner State	Southwest
Oregon	1859 (33)	Salem	97,132/251,571	3,421,399	Beaver State	West
Pennsylvania	1787 (2)	Harrisburg	46,058/119,291	12,281,054	Keystone State	Mid-Atlantic
Rhode Island	1790 (13)	Providence	1,231/3,189	1,048,319	Ocean State	New England
South Carolina	1788 (8)	Columbia	31,189/80,779	4,012,012	Palmetto State	Southeast
South Dakota	1889 (40)	Pierre	77,121/199,744	754,844	Mount Rushmore State; Coyote State	Midwest
Tennessee	1796 (16)	Nashville	42,146/109,158	5,689,283	Volunteer State	Southeast
Texas	1845 (28)	Austin	267,277/692,248	20,851,820	Lone Star State	Southwest
Utah	1896 (45)	Salt Lake City	84,904/219,902	2,233,169	Beehive State	West
Vermont	1791 (14)	Montpelier	9,615/24,903	608,827	Green Mountain State	New England
Virginia	1788 (10)	Richmond	42,326/109,625	7,078,515	Old Dominion	Southeast
Washington	1889 (42)	Olympia	70,637/182,949	5,894,121	Evergreen State	West
West Virginia	1863 (35)	Charleston	24,231/62,759	1,808,344	Mountain State	Southeast
Wisconsin	1848 (30)	Madison	65,499/169,643	5,363,675	Badger State	Midwest
Wyoming	1890 (44)	Cheyenne	97,818/253,349	493,782	Equality State	West

Total area: Data from 1990 as reported in *Statistical Abstract of the United States*, 2000.
Resident population: U.S. Department of Commerce, U.S. Census Bureau.

APPENDIX B

Countries of the World

Country	Area sq mi/sq km	Population	Capital	Major languages	Continent
Afghanistan	251,772/652,089	24,800,000	Kabul	Pashtu and Afghan Persian	Asia
Albania	10,579/27,400	3,300,000	Tiranë	Albanian and Greek	Europe
Algeria	919,590/2,381,738	30,200,000	Algiers	Arabic, Berber, and French	Africa
Andorra	185/479	54,000	Andorra la Vella	Catalan, French, and Castilian Spanish	Europe
Angola	481,350/1,246,697	12,000,000	Luanda	Portuguese and Bantu	Africa
Antigua and Barbuda	170/440	100,000	St. John's	English	North America
Argentina	1,056,640/2,736,698	36,100,000	Buenos Aires	Spanish, English, and Italian	South America
Armenia	10,888/28,200	3,800,000	Yerevan	Armenian	Asia
Australia	2,951,521/7,644,439	18,700,000	Canberra	English and aboriginal languages	Australia
Austria	31,942/82,729	8,100,000	Vienna	German	Europe
Azerbaijan	33,436/86,599	7,700,000	Baku	Azeri, Russian, and Armenian	Asia
The Bahamas	3,860/9,997	300,000	Nassau	English and Creole	North America
Bahrain	266/689	600,000	Manama	Arabic, English, Farsi, and Urdu	Asia
Bangladesh	50,260/130,173	123,400,000	Dhaka	Bangla and English	Asia
Barbados	166/430	300,000	Bridgetown	English	North America
Belarus	80,108/207,480	10,200,000	Minsk	Byelorussian and Russian	Europe
Belgium	11,790/30,536	10,200,000	Brussels	Flemish and French	Europe
Belize	8,800/22,792	200,000	Belmopan	English and Spanish	North America
Benin	42,710/110,619	6,000,000	Porto-Novo	French and Fon	Africa
Bhutan	18,150/47,009	800,000	Thimphu	Dzongkha and Nepali	Asia
Bolivia	418,680/1,084,381	8,000,000	Sucre (judicial) and La Paz (administrative)	Spanish	South America

Country	Area (sq mi/sq km)	Population	Capital	Language(s)	Continent
Bosnia and Herzegovina	16,691/43,320	4,000,000	Sarejevo	Serbo-Croatian	Europe
Botswana	218,810/566,718	1,400,000	Gaborone	English and Setswana	Africa
Brazil	3,265,060/8,456,505	162,100,000	Brasília	Portuguese, Spanish, French, and English	South America
Brunei	2,035/5,271	300,000	Bandar Seri Begawan	Malay, English, and Chinese	Asia
Bulgaria	42,683/110,548	8,300,000	Sofia	Bulgarian	Europe
Burkina Faso	105,637/273,763	11,300,000	Ouagadougou	French and Sudanic languages	Africa
Burundi	9,900/25,641	5,500,000	Bujumbura	Kurund, French, and Swahili	Africa
Cambodia	68,154/176,519	10,800,000	Phnom Penh	Khmer and French	Asia
Cameroon	179,690/465,397	14,300,000	Yaoundé	English and French	Africa
Canada	3,849,674/9,970,610	31,000,000	Ottawa	English and French	North America
Cape Verde	1,560/4,040	400,000	Praia	Portuguese	Africa
Central African Republic	240,530/622,973	3,400,000	Bangui	French and Sango	Africa
Chad	486,180/1,259,206	7,400,000	N'Djamena	French and Arabic	Africa
Chile	289,110/748,795	14,800,000	Santiago	Spanish	South America
China	3,600,930/9,326,409	1,242,500,000	Beijing	Mandarin and local Chinese dialects	Asia
Colombia	401,040/1,038,694	38,600,000	Bogotá	Spanish	South America
Comoros	860/2,227	500,000	Moroni	French, Arabic, and Comoran	Africa
Congo Republic	131,850/341,492	2,700,000	Brazzaville	French, Kikongo, Lingala, and other African languages	Africa
Costa Rica	19,710/51,049	3,500,000	San José	Spanish and English	North America
Côte d'Ivoire (Ivory Coast)	122,780/318,000	15,600,000	Yamoussoukro	French and many African languages	Africa
Croatia	21,590/55,918	4,200,000	Zagreb	Serbo-Croatian	Europe
Cuba	42,400/109,816	11,100,000	Havana	Spanish	North America
Cyprus	3,568/9,242	700,000	Nicosia	Greek	Asia

Country	Area sq mi/sq km	Population	Capital	Major languages	Continent
Czech Republic	29,838/77,280	10,300,000	Prague	Czech and Slovak	Europe
Democratic Republic of Congo	875,309/2,267,050	49,000,000	Kinshasa	French, English, Swahili, Lingala, and other Bantu dialects	Africa
Denmark	16,320/42,269	5,300,000	Copenhagen	Danish and Faroese	Europe
Djibouti	8,950/23,181	700,000	Djibouti	Arabic and French	Africa
Dominica	290/751	100,000	Roseau	English and Creole	North America
Dominican Republic	18,680/48,381	8,300,000	Santo Domingo	Spanish	North America
Ecuador	106,890/276,845	12,200,000	Quito	Spanish and Quechua	South America
Egypt	384,444/995,450	65,500,000	Cairo	Arabic, English, and French	Africa
El Salvador	8,000/20,720	5,800,000	San Salvador	Spanish and Nahua	North America
Equatorial Guinea	10,830/28,050	400,000	Malabo	Spanish, Fang, and Bubi	Africa
Eritrea	38,996/101,000	3,800,000	Asmara	Tigrinya and Arabic	Africa
Estonia	16,320/42,269	1,400,000	Tallinn	Estonian, Latvian, Lithuanian, and Russian	Europe
Ethiopia	386,100/1,000,000	58,400,000	Addis Ababa	Amharic, English, and local languages	Africa
Fiji	7,054/18,270	800,000	Suva	Fijian, Hindi, and English	Islands in the Pacific Ocean
Finland	117,602/304,590	5,200,000	Helsinki	Finnish and Swedish	Europe
France	212,392/550,095	58,800,000	Paris	French	Europe
Gabon	99,490/257,679	1,200,000	Libreville	French, Fang, and Bantu dialects	Africa
Gambia	3,860/9,997	1,200,000	Banjul	English and Mandinka	Africa
Georgia	26,911/69,699	5,400,000	Tbilisi	Georgian and Russian	Asia
Germany	134,853/349,270	82,300,000	Berlin	German	Europe
Ghana	87,583/226,840	18,900,000	Accra	English and African languages	Africa

Country	Area (sq mi/sq km)	Population	Capital	Language	Continent
Greece	49,768/128,900	10,500,000	Athens	Greek	Europe
Grenada	130/337	100,000	St. George's	English and French patois	North America
Guatemala	41,860/108,417	11,600,000	Guatemala City	Spanish and Mayan dialects	North America
Guinea	94,873/245,721	7,500,000	Conakry	French, Soussou, and Manika	Africa
Guinea-Bissau	10,860/28,127	1,100,000	Bissau	Portuguese and Crioulo	Africa
Guyana	76,000/196,840	700,000	Georgetown	English, Hindi, and Urdu	South America
Haiti	10,640/27,558	7,500,000	Port-au-Prince	French and French Creole	North America
Honduras	43,200/111,888	5,900,000	Tegucigalpa	Spanish	North America
Hungary	35,363/92,431	10,100,000	Budapest	Hungarian	Europe
Iceland	38,707/100,251	300,000	Reykjavik	Icelandic	Europe
India	1,147,950/2,973,191	988,700,000	New Dehli	Hindi, English, and 14 other official languages	Asia
Indonesia	705,190/1,826,442	207,400,000	Jakarta	Bahasa	Asia
Iran	631,660/1,635,999	64,100,000	Tehran	Farsi, Turkic, and Kurdish	Asia
Iraq	168,870/437,373	21,800,000	Baghdad	Arabic and Kurdish	Asia
Ireland	26,598/68,890	3,700,000	Dublin	English and Irish	Europe
Israel	7,961/20,619	6,000,000	Jerusalem	Hebrew and Arabic	Asia
Italy	113,351/293,594	57,700,000	Rome	Italian	Europe
Jamaica	4,180/10,826	2,600,000	Kingston	English and Jamaican Creole	North America
Japan	145,370/376,508	126,400,000	Tokyo	Japanese	Asia
Jordan	34,336/88,930	4,600,000	Amman	Arabic	Asia
Kazakhstan	1,031,170/2,670,730	15,600,000	Almaty	Kazakh and Russian	Asia
Kenya	219,745/569,139	28,300,000	Nairobi	English and Swahili	Africa
Kiribati	313/811	82,449	Tarawa	Gilbertese and English	Islands in the Pacific Ocean
North Korea	46,490/120,409	22,200,000	Pyongyang	Korean	Asia
South Korea	38,120/98,731	46,400,000	Seoul	Korean	Asia

Country	Area sq mi/sq km	Population	Capital	Major languages	Continent
Kuwait	6,880/17,819	1,900,000	Kuwait City	Arabic	Asia
Kyrgyzstan	74,054/191,800	4,700,000	Bishkek	Kyrgyz and Russian	Asia
Laos	89,110/230,795	5,300,000	Vientiane	Lao, French, and English	Asia
Latvia	23,598/62,051	2,400,000	Riga	Latvian and English	Europe
Lebanon	3,950/10,231	4,100,000	Beirut	Arabic and French	Asia
Lesotho	11,720/30,355	2,100,000	Maseru	Sesotho and English	Africa
Liberia	37,190/96,322	2,800,000	Monrovia	English and Niger-Congo languages	Africa
Libya	679,360/1,759,542	5,700,000	Tripoli	Arabic, Italian, and English	Africa
Liechtenstein	60/155	30,000	Vaduz	German	Europe
Lithuania	25,019/64,799	3,700,000	Vilnius	Lithuanian, Russian, and Polish	Europe
Luxembourg	1,000/2,590	400,000	Luxembourg	Luxembourgisch, German, French, and English	Europe
Macedonia	9,819/25,431	2,000,000	Skopje	Macedonian	Europe
Madagascar	224,530/581,533	14,000,000	Antananarivo	French and Malagasy	Africa
Malawi	36,320/94,069	9,800,000	Lilongwe	English and Chichewa	Africa
Malaysia	126,850/328,542	22,200,000	Kuala Lumpur	Malay, English, and Chinese dialects	Asia
Maldives	116/300	300,000	Male	Divehi	Asia
Mali	471,120/1,220,201	10,100,000	Bamako	Bambura and French	Africa
Malta	120/311	400,000	Valletta	Maltese and English	Europe
Marshall Islands	70/181	100,000	Majuro	English, Marshallese dialects, and Japanese	Islands in the Pacific Ocean
Mauritania	395,840/1,025,226	2,500,000	Nouakchott	Arabic and Wolof	Africa
Mauritius	784/2,030	1,200,000	Port Louis	English, Creole, and French	Africa
Mexico	736,950/1,908,700	97,500,000	Mexico City	Spanish	North America

Country	Area (sq mi/sq km)	Population	Capital	Languages	Location
Micronesia	270/699	100,000	Palikir	English, Trukese, Yapese, and Kosrean	Islands in the Pacific Ocean
Moldova	12,730/32,971	4,200,000	Kishinev	Moldovan, Russian, and Gagauz	Europe
Monaco	.6/1.6	30,000	Monaco	French, Monégasque, and English	Europe
Mongolia	604,825/1,566,500	2,400,000	Ulaabaatar	Khalkha, Mongolian, Turkic, Russian, and Chinese	Asia
Morocco	173,320/446,309	28,600,000	Rabat	Arabic, Berber, and French	Africa
Mozambique	302,740/784,097	18,600,000	Maputo	Portuguese and African languages	Africa
Myanmar	253,880/657,549	47,100,000	Yangon	Burmese	Asia
Namibia	317,870/823,283	1,600,000	Windhoek	English, Afrikaans, and German	Africa
Nauru	21/54	10,390	Yaren	Nauruan and English	Island in the Pacific
Nepal	52,820/136,804	23,700,000	Kathmandu	Nepali	Asia
Netherlands	13,097/33,921	15,700,000	Amsterdam	Dutch	Europe
New Zealand	103,420/267,987	3,800,000	Wellington	English and Maori	Islands in the Pacific Ocean
Nicaragua	46,873/121,401	4,800,000	Managua	Spanish	North America
Niger	489,070/1,266,691	10,100,000	Niamey	French, Hausa, and Djerma	Africa
Nigeria	351,650/910,774	121,800,000	Abuja	English, Hausa, Yoruba, Ibo, and Fulani	Africa
Norway	118,467/306,830	4,400,000	Oslo	Norwegian	Europe
Oman	82,030/212,458	2,500,000	Muscat	Arabic	Asia
Pakistan	297,640/770,888	141,900,000	Islamabad	Urdu, Punjabi, and English	Asia
Palau	190/492	20,000	Koror	Palauan and English	Islands in the Pacific Ocean
Panama	28,737/74,428	2,800,000	Panama City	Spanish and English	North America
Papua New Guinea	174,850/452,862	4,300,000	Port Moresby	Pidgin English, English, and Motu	Islands in the Pacific Ocean
Paraguay	153,400/397,306	5,200,000	Asunción	Spanish and Guarani	South America
Peru	494,210/1,280,044	26,100,000	Lima	Spanish, Quechua, and Aymará	South America
Philippines	115,120/298,161	75,300,000	Manila	Filipino, Tagalog, and English	Asia

Country	Area sq mi/sq km	Population	Capital	Major languages	Continent
Poland	117,537/304,420	38,700,000	Warsaw	Polish	Europe
Portugal	35,502/91,950	10,000,000	Lisbon	Portuguese	Europe
Qatar	4,250/11,008	500,000	Doha	Arabic and English	Asia
Romania	88,934/230,339	22,500,000	Bucharest	Romanian, Hungarian, and German	Europe
Russia	6,520,656/16,888,499	147,000,000	Moscow	Russian	Europe and Asia
Rwanda	9,525/24,670	8,000,000	Kigali	Kinyarwanda, French, and Kiswahili	Africa
St. Kitts and Nevis	140/363	40,000	Basseterre	English	North America
St. Lucia	236/611	100,000	Castries	English and French patois	North America
St. Vincent and the Grenadines	150/389	100,000	Kingstown	English	North America
Samoa	1,090/2,823	200,000	Apia	Samoan and English	Islands in the Pacific Ocean
San Marino	20/52	20,000	San Marino	Italian	Europe
São Tomé and Principe	293/759	200,000	São Tomé	Portuguese	Africa
Saudi Arabia	830,000/2,149,700	20,200,000	Riyadh	Arabic	Asia
Senegal	74,340/192,541	9,000,000	Dakar	French and Wolof	Africa
Seychelles	174/451	100,000	Victoria	Creole, English, and French	Africa
Sierra Leone	27,650/71,614	4,600,000	Freetown	English, Mende, Temne, and Krio	Africa
Singapore	236/611	3,900,000	Singapore	Chinese, English, Malay and Tamil	Asia
Slovakia	18,564/48,080	5,400,000	Bratislava	Slovak and Hungarian	Europe
Slovenia	7,768/20,119	2,000,000	Ljubljana	Slovenian	Europe
Solomon Islands	10,810/27,998	400,000	Honiara	English, Pidgin English, and Melanesian	Islands in the Pacific Ocean
Somalia	242,220/627,350	10,700,000	Mogadishu	Somali and Arabic	Africa
South Africa	471,440/1,221,030	38,900,000	Pretoria, Cape Town, and Bloemfontein	Afrikaans, English, Zulu, and other African languages	Africa

Country					
Spain	192,834/499,440	39,400,000	Madrid	Spanish and Catalan	Europe
Sri Lanka	24,950/64,621	18,900,000	Colombo	Sinhala, Tamil, and English	Asia
Sudan	917,375/2,376,000	28,500,000	Khartoum	Arabic, Nubian, and Sudanic languages	Africa
Suriname	60,230/155,996	400,000	Paramaribo	Dutch, English, and Hindi	South America
Swaziland	6,640/17,198	1,000,000	Mbabane	Siswati and English	Africa
Sweden	158,927/411,621	8,900,000	Stockholm	Swedish	Europe
Switzerland	15,270/39,590	7,100,000	Bern	German, French, Italian, and Romansch	Europe
Syria	70,958/183,781	15,600,000	Damascus	Arabic and Kurdish	Asia
Taiwan	13,970/36,182	21,700,000	Taipei	Mandarin, Taiwanese, and Hakka dialects	Asia
Tajikstan	54,286/140,601	6,100,000	Dushanbe	Tajik and Russian	Asia
Tanzania	341,154/883,588	30,600,000	Dar es Salaam	Swahili and English	Africa
Thailand	197,250/510,878	61,100,000	Bangkok	Thai and English	Asia
Togo	21,000/54,390	4,900,000	Lomé	French, Kabye, Ewe, Mina, and Dagomba	Africa
Tonga	290/751	107,335	Nuku'alofa	Tongan and English	Islands in the Pacific Ocean
Trinidad and Tobago	1,980/5,128	1,300,000	Port-of-Spain	English, Hindi, and French	North America
Tunisia	59,980/155,348	9,500,000	Tunis	Arabic and French	Africa
Turkey	297,150/769,619	64,800,000	Ankara	Turkish, Kurdish, and Arabic	Asia and Europe
Turkmenistan	181,440/470,000	4,700,000	Ashgabat	Turkmen, Russian, and Uzbek	Asia
Tuvalu	9/23	10,297	Funafuti	Tuvaluan and English	Islands in the Pacific Ocean
Uganda	77,085/199,650	21,000,000	Kampala	English, Luganda, Swahili, and Bantu languages	Africa
Ukraine	223,687/579,349	50,300,000	Kiev	Ukranian, Russian, Romanian, and Polish	Europe

Country	Area sq mi/sq km	Population	Capital	Major languages	Continent
United Arab Emirates	32,280/83,605	2,700,000	Abu Dhabi	Arabic, Persian, English, Hindi, and Urdu	Asia
United Kingdom	93,282/241,600	59,100,000	London	English, Welsh, and Scottish Gaelic	Europe
United States	3,536,340/9,159,121	270,200,000	Washington, D.C.	English and Spanish	North America
Uruguay	67,490/174,499	3,200,000	Montevideo	Spanish and Brazilero	South America
Uzbekistan	159,938/414,356	24,100,000	Tashkent	Uzbek, Russian, and Tajik	Asia
Vanuatu	4,710/12,199	200,000	Port-Vila	Bislama, English, and French	Islands in the Pacific Ocean
Vatican City (The Holy See)	.2/.4	1,000	Vatican City	Italian and Latin	Europe
Venezuela	340,560/882,050	23,300,000	Caracas	Spanish and Indian dialects	South America
Vietnam	126,670/325,485	78,500,000	Hanoi	Vietnamese, French, Chinese, English, and Khmer	Asia
Yemen	203,850/527,972	15,800,000	San'a	Arabic	Asia
Yugoslavia	39,382/102,000	10,600,000	Belgrade	Serbo-Croatian and Albanian	Europe
Zambia	287,020/743,382	9,500,000	Lusaka	English and about 70 Bantu dialects	Africa
Zimbabwe	149,363/386,850	11,000,000	Harare	English, Shona, and Sindebele	Africa

APPENDIX C

Atlas

When you look at maps with your child, please remember that, because the world is constantly in flux, international borders and even names of countries change from time to time.

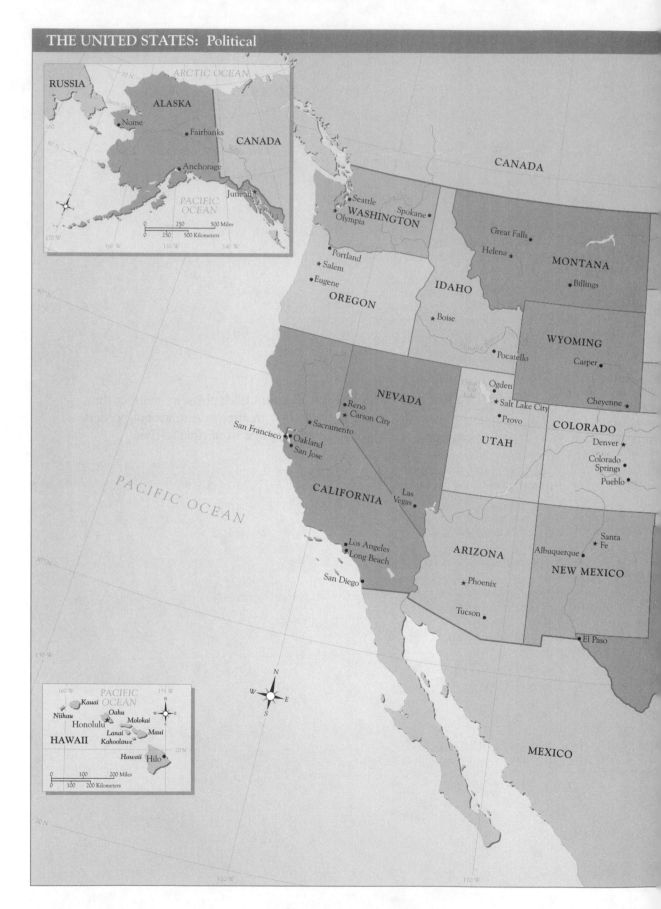

THE UNITED STATES: Political

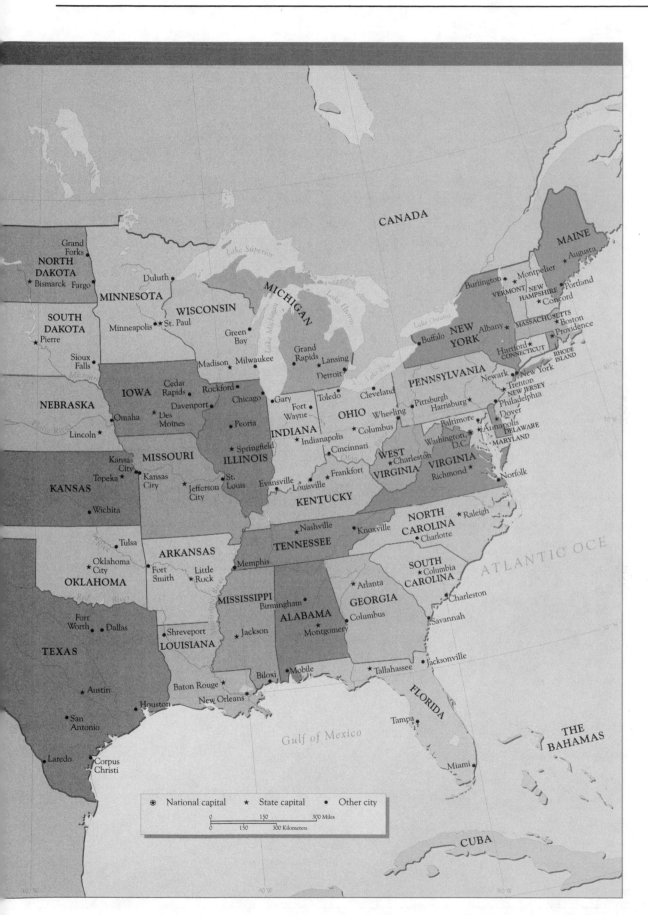

THE UNITED STATES: Physical

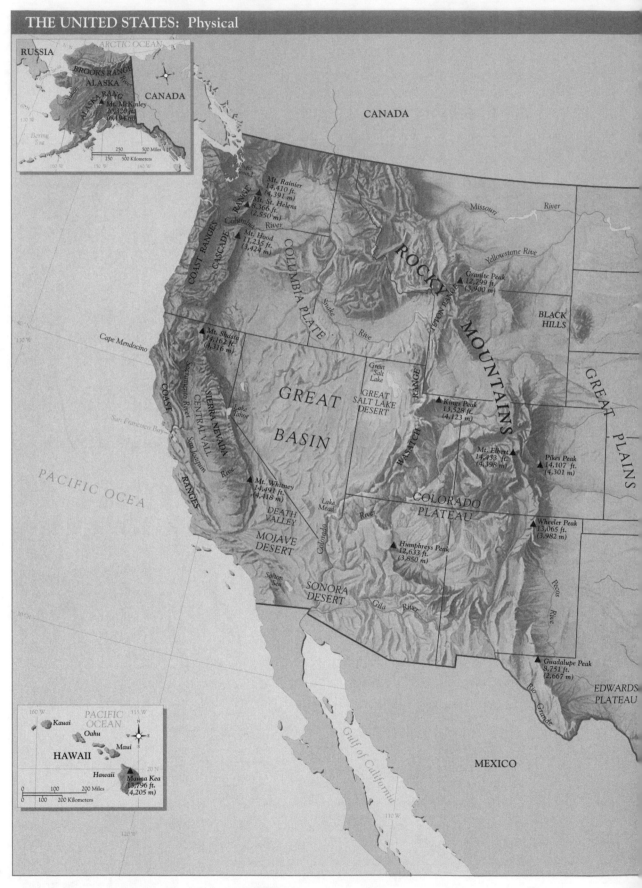

RUSSIA

ARCTIC OCEAN

BROOKS RANGE

ALASKA

ALASKA RANG

CANADA

Mt. McKinley
20,320 ft.
(6,194 m)

Bering
Sea

250   500 Miles

250   500 Kilometers

CANADA

Puget
Sound

Mt. Rainier
14,410 ft.
(4,391 m)

Mt. St. Helens
8,366 ft.
(2,550 m)

Columbia   River

Mt. Hood
11,235 ft.
(3,424 m)

COAST RANGES

CASCADE RANGE

COLUMBIA PLATEAU

ROCKY MOUNTAINS

Missouri   River

Yellowstone Rive

Granite Peak
12,799 ft.
(3,900 m)

BLACK
HILLS

Snake
Rive

TETON RANGE

Cape Mendocino

Mt. Shasta
4,162 ft.
(4,316 m)

Sacramento River

COAST

SIERRA NEVADA

CENTRAL VALL

San Francisco Bay

Lake
Tahoe

Great
Salt
Lake

GREAT
SALT LAKE
DESERT

WASATCH RANGE

GREAT
BASIN

GREAT PLAINS

Kings Peak
13,528 ft.
(4,123 m)

San Joaquin   River

Mt. Elbert
14,433 ft.
(4,398 m)

Pikes Peak
14,107 ft.
(4,301 m)

PACIFIC OCEA

RANGES

Mt. Whitney
14,491 ft.
(4,418 m)

DEATH
VALLEY

MOJAVE
DESERT

Lake
Mead

River

COLORADO
PLATEAU

Wheeler Peak
13,065 ft.
(3,982 m)

Colorado

Humphreys Peak
12,633 ft.
(3,850 m)

Salton
Sea

SONORA
DESERT

Gila   River

Pecos   River

Guadalupe Peak
8,751 ft.
(2,667 m)

EDWARDS
PLATEAU

160 W   155 W

Kauai

PACIFIC
OCEAN

Oahu

Maui

HAWAII

Hawaii

Mauna Kea
13,796 ft.
(4,205 m)

20 N

100   200 Miles

100   200 Kilometers

Rio Grande

Gulf of California

MEXICO

110 W

120 W

CANADA

Lake of
the Woods

Lake Superior

GREAT

MESABI RANGE

LAKES

Lake Huron

CENTRAL PLAINS

Mississippi

River

Lake Michigan

Lake Erie

Lake Ontario

ADIRONDACK
MTS

ALLEGHENY
PLATEAU

St. Lawrence River

WHITE MTS

Mt. Washington
6,288 ft.
(1,917 m)

GREEN MTS

Cape Cod

Hudson River

Long Island

Platte River

Missouri

River

Wabash
River

Ohio

River

ALLEGHENY MOUNTAINS

APPALACHIAN MOUNTAINS

Susquehanna

River

Potomac River

Delaware Bay

70° W

Chesapeake Bay

INTERIOR PLAINS

Arkansas

River

OZARK
PLATEAU

OUACHITA
MOUNTAINS

Red

River

Mississippi

River

River

Tennessee

River

Mt. Mitchell
6,684 ft.
(2,037 m)

PIEDMONT

Savannah River

Cape Hatteras

ATLANTIC COASTAL PLAIN

ATLANTIC OCE

Breczos

River

Colorado River

GULF COASTAL PLAIN

Galveston Bay

Mobile Bay

Mississippi Delta

Alabama

River

Chattahoochee

Gulf of Mexico

Lake
Okeechobee

Bahama Islands

N
W   E
S

0   150   300 Miles
0   150   300 Kilometers

Florida Key

Straits of Florida

CUBA

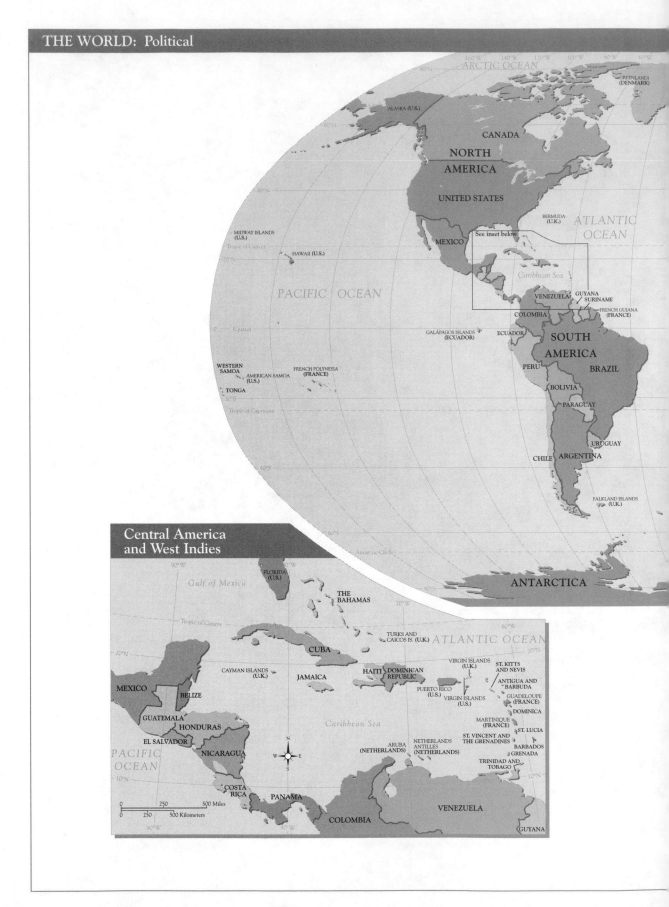

THE WORLD: Political

Central America and West Indies

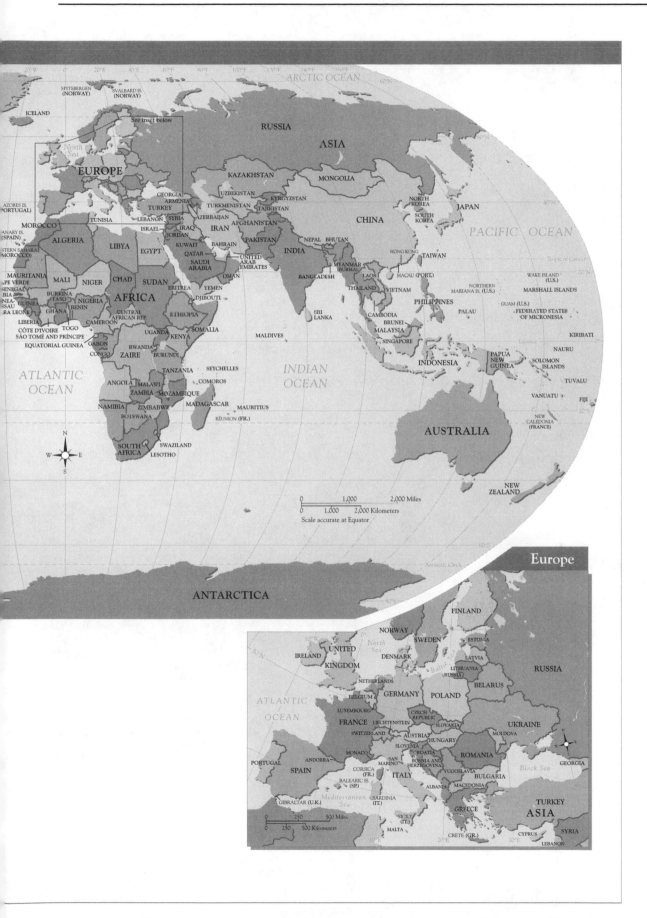

THE WORLD: Physical

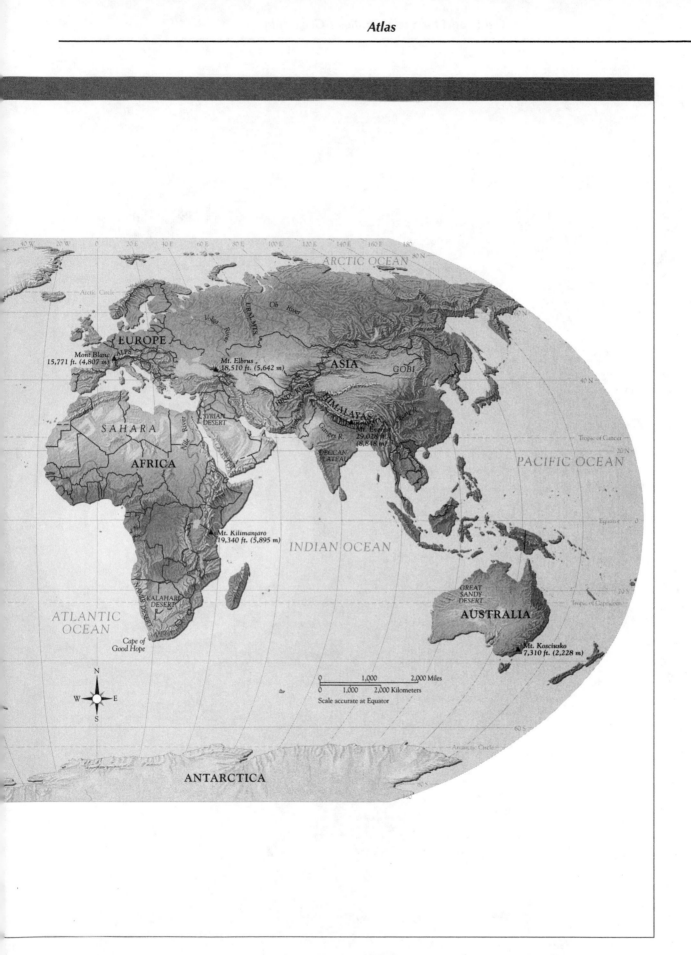

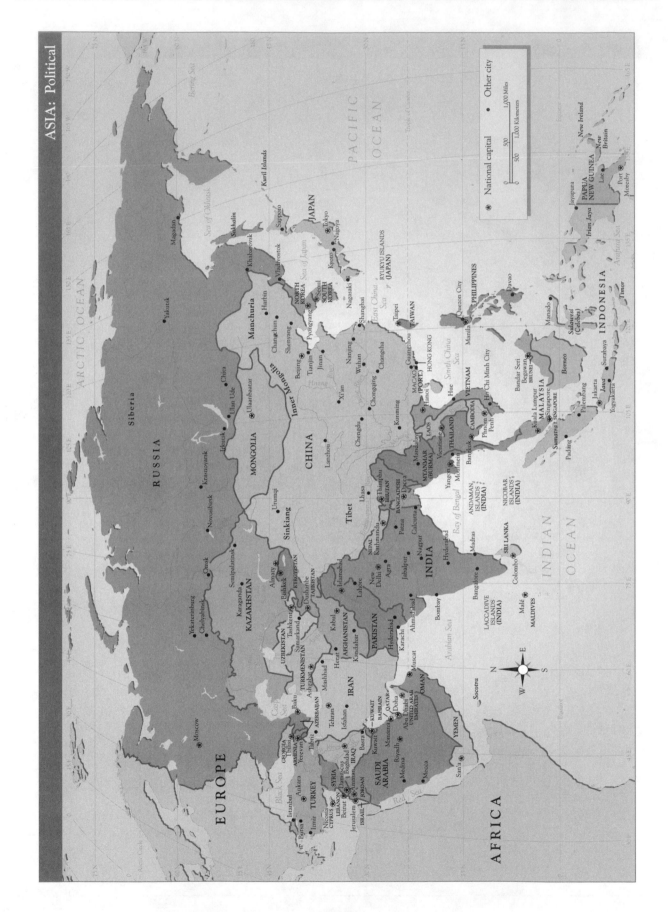

ASIA: Political

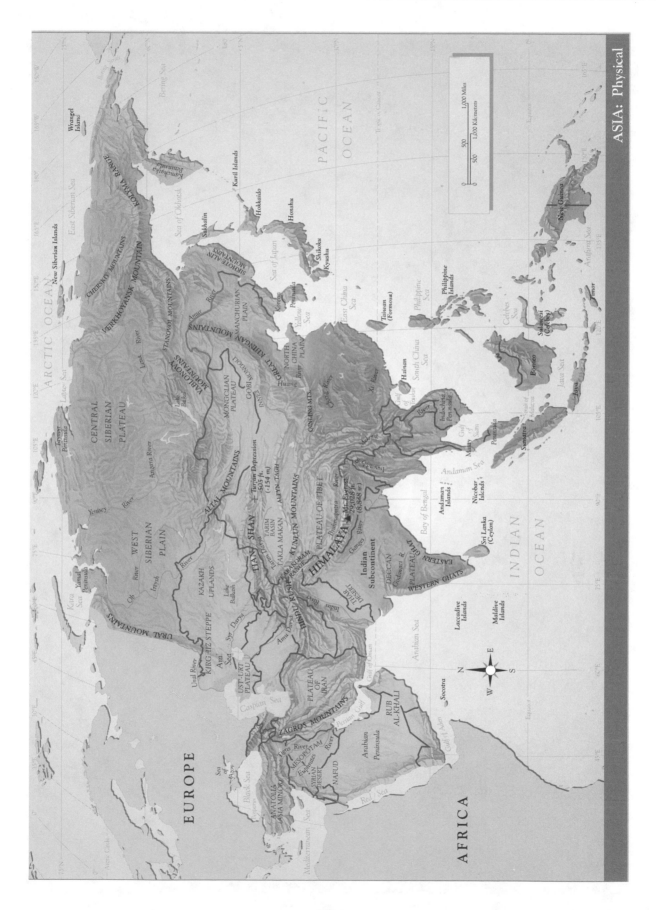

ASIA: Physical

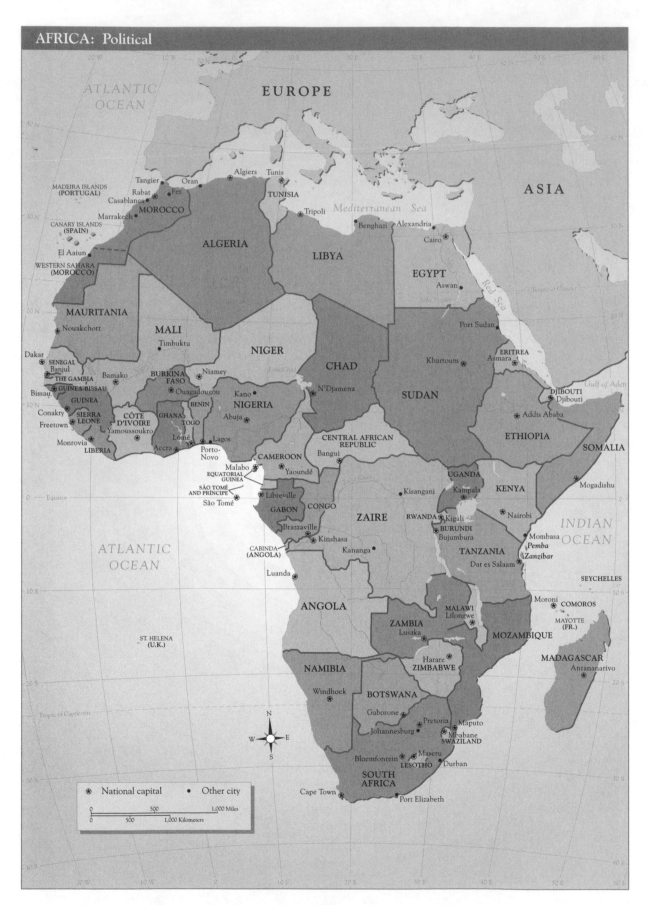

AFRICA: Political

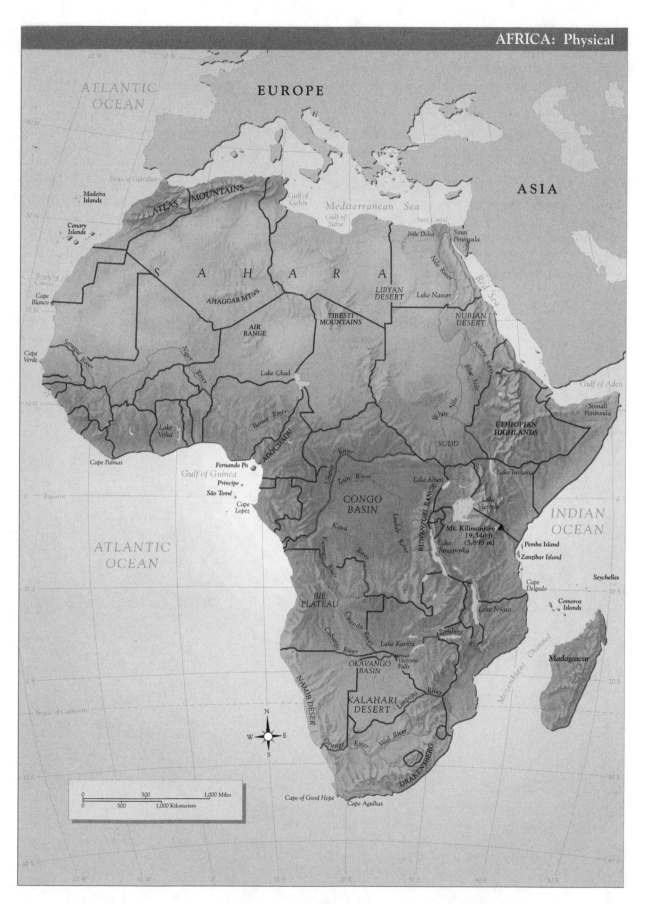

AFRICA: Physical

ATLANTIC OCEAN

EUROPE

ASIA

Strait of Gibraltar

Madeira Islands

ATLAS MOUNTAINS

Gulf of Gabes

Mediterranean Sea

Gulf of Sidra

Suez Canal

Canary Islands

Tropic of Cancer

Cape Blanco

S A H A R A

AHAGGAR MTNS

AIR RANGE

Nile Delta

Sinai Peninsula

Nile River

LIBYAN DESERT

Lake Nasser

TIBESTI MOUNTAINS

NUBIAN DESERT

Red Sea

Senegal River

Cape Verde

Niger River

Lake Chad

Atbara River

Blue Nile

Gulf of Aden

Benue River

Lake Volta

White Nile

SUDD

ETHIOPIAN HIGHLANDS

Somali Peninsula

Cape Palmas

Gulf of Guinea

Fernando Po

Príncipe

São Tomé

Cape Lopez

ADOUMAOU

Ubangi River

Zaire River

CONGO BASIN

Kasai

Lake Albert

RUWENZORI RANGE

Lake Victoria

Lualaba River

Mt. Kilimanjaro 19,340 ft. (5,895 m)

Lake Turkana

INDIAN OCEAN

Equator

Kwango River

ATLANTIC OCEAN

BIÉ PLATEAU

Cuanza River

Lake Tanganyika

Pemba Island

Zanzibar Island

Seychelles

Cape Delgado

Comoros Islands

Cubango River

OKAVANGO BASIN

Lake Kariba

Victoria Falls

Zambezi River

Lake Nyasa

NAMIB DESERT

KALAHARI DESERT

Limpopo River

Mozambique Channel

Madagascar

Tropic of Capricorn

N
W   E
S

Orange River

Vaal River

DRAKENSBERG

Cape of Good Hope

Cape Agulhas

0   500   1,000 Miles
0   500   1,000 Kilometers

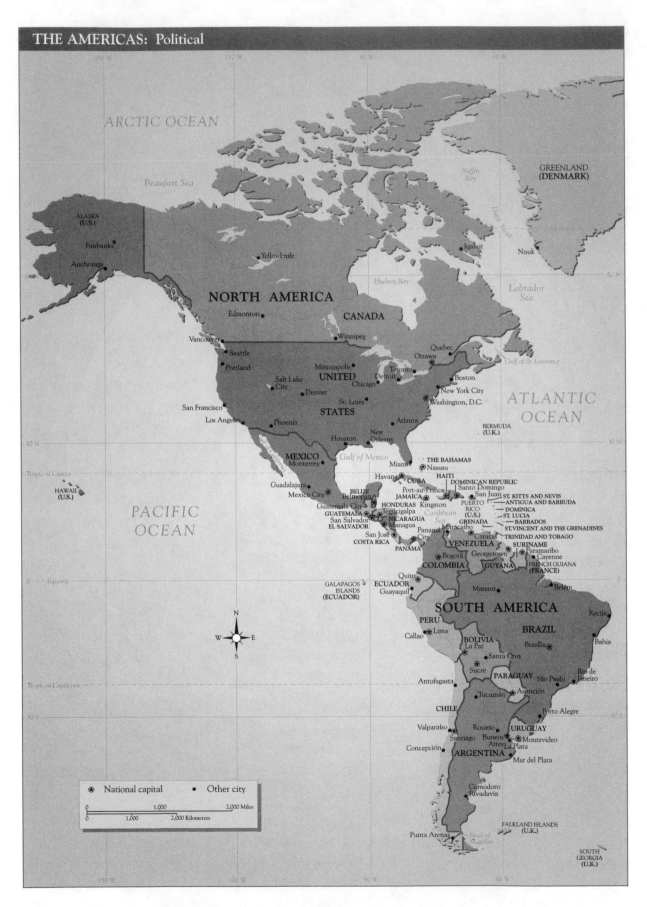

THE AMERICAS: Political

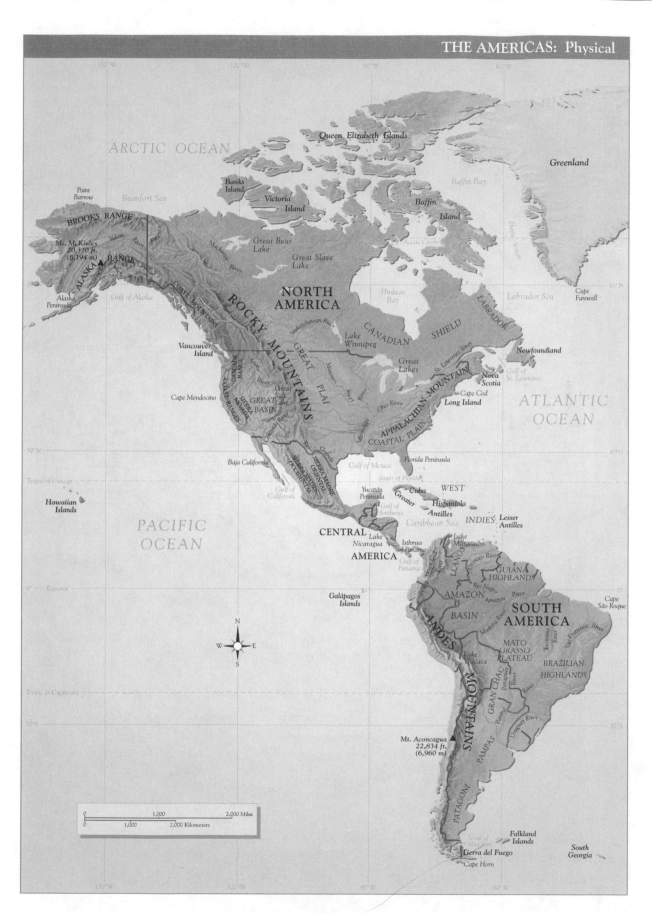

THE AMERICAS: Physical

ARCTIC OCEAN

Queen Elizabeth Islands

Greenland

Point Barrow

Beaufort Sea

Banks Island

Baffin Bay

BROOKS RANGE

Victoria Island

Mt. McKinley 20,320 ft. (6,194 m)

Baffin Island

ALASKA RANGE

Yukon River

Great Bear Lake

Mackenzie River

Great Slave Lake

Davis Strait

Cape Farewell

Alaska Peninsula

Gulf of Alaska

COAST MOUNTAINS

NORTH AMERICA

Hudson Bay

Arctic Circle

Labrador Sea

Vancouver Island

Saskatchewan River

Lake Winnipeg

CANADIAN SHIELD

LABRADOR

ROCKY MOUNTAINS

GREAT PLAINS

Missouri River

Great Lakes

St. Lawrence River

Newfoundland

Gulf of St. Lawrence

Snake River

Cape Mendocino

CASCADE RANGE

COAST RANGES

SIERRA NEVADA

Great Salt Lake

GREAT BASIN

Colorado River

Ohio River

APPALACHIAN MOUNTAIN

Nova Scotia

Cape Cod

Long Island

ATLANTIC OCEAN

Mississippi River

Red River

COASTAL PLAIN

Baja California

SIERRA MADRE OCCIDENTAL

SIERRA MADRE ORIENTAL

Rio Grande

Gulf of Mexico

Florida Peninsula

Strait of Florida

Tropic of Cancer

Hawaiian Islands

Gulf of California

Yucatán Peninsula

Gulf of Honduras

Cuba

Greater Antilles

Hispaniola

WEST INDIES

Lesser Antilles

PACIFIC OCEAN

CENTRAL

Lake Nicaragua

Caribbean Sea

AMERICA

Isthmus of Panama

Gulf of Panama

Lake Maracaibo

Magdalena River

LLANOS

Orinoco River

GUIANA HIGHLANDS

Galápagos Islands

Equator

AMAZON BASIN

Rio Negro

Amazon River

SOUTH AMERICA

Cape São Roque

ANDES

Madeira River

MATO GROSSO PLATEAU

Tapajós River

São Francisco River

BRAZILIAN HIGHLANDS

Lake Titicaca

GRAN CHACO

Paraguay River

Paraná River

PAMPAS

Uruguay River

Mt. Aconcagua 22,834 ft. (6,960 m)

Tropic of Capricorn

MOUNTAINS

PATAGONIA

Falkland Islands

South Georgia

Strait of Magellan

Tierra del Fuego

Cape Horn

N W E S

0   1,000   2,000 Miles
0   1,000   2,000 Kilometers

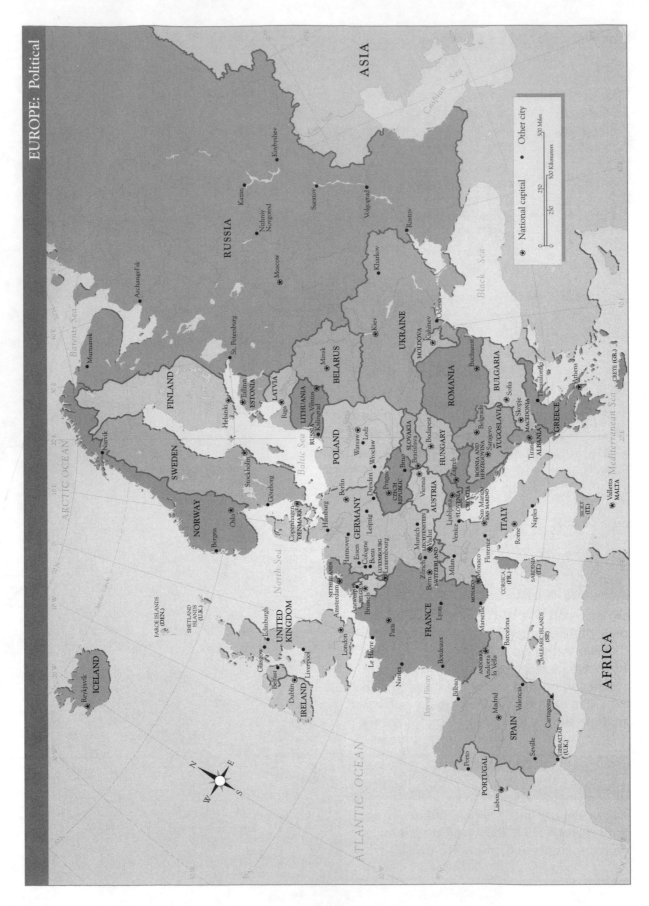

EUROPE: Political

ASIA

RUSSIA

Kazan

Nizhniy Novgorod

Samara

Kuybyshev

Moscow

Volgograd

Rostov

Archangelsk

Murmansk

Kharkov

Kiev

UKRAINE

MOLDOVA

Kishinev

Odessa

Black Sea

St. Petersburg

Minsk

BELARUS

FINLAND

Helsinki

ESTONIA

Tallinn

LATVIA

Riga

LITHUANIA

Vilnius

RUSSIA

Kaliningrad

Bucharest

BULGARIA

ROMANIA

Sofia

Thessaloniki

MACEDONIA

Skopje

GREECE

Athens

Belgrade

YUGOSLAVIA

Tirane

ALBANIA

CRETE (GR.)

Valletta

MALTA

Mediterranean Sea

SWEDEN

NORWAY

Narvik

Stockholm

Göteborg

Oslo

Bergen

POLAND

Warsaw

Lodz

Wroclaw

Brno

SLOVAKIA

Bratislava

HUNGARY

Budapest

Zagreb

CROATIA

SLOVENIA

Ljubljana

BOSNIA AND HERZEGOVINA

Sarajevo

Copenhagen

DENMARK

Hamburg

Berlin

Dresden

Leipzig

GERMANY

Hannover

Essen

Cologne

Bonn

Prague

CZECH REPUBLIC

Vienna

AUSTRIA

LIECHTENSTEIN

Vaduz

Munich

Baltic Sea

Zurich

Bern

SWITZERLAND

Venice

Milan

San Marino

SAN MARINO

ITALY

Florence

Rome

Naples

SICILY (IT.)

SARDINIA (IT.)

North Sea

NETHERLANDS

Amsterdam

Antwerp

BELGIUM

Brussels

LUXEMBOURG

Luxembourg

FRANCE

Lyon

Monaco

MONACO

Marseille

CORSICA (FR.)

UNITED KINGDOM

Edinburgh

Glasgow

Belfast

Dublin

IRELAND

London

Liverpool

Le Havre

Paris

Nantes

Bordeaux

SHETLAND ISLANDS (U.K.)

FAROE ISLANDS (DEN.)

Bay of Biscay

Arctic Circle

ATLANTIC OCEAN

ICELAND

Reykjavik

ARCTIC OCEAN

Barents Sea

ANDORRA

Andorra la Vella

SPAIN

Madrid

Barcelona

Valencia

Bilbao

BALEARIC ISLANDS (SP.)

GIBRALTAR (U.K.)

Cartagena

Seville

PORTUGAL

Lisbon

Porto

AFRICA

Caspian Sea

National capital

Other city

0   250   500 Miles

0   250   500 Kilometers

N

S

E

W

146

EUROPE: Physical

Answers to "Fact Checkers"

Chapter 1

1. Mesopotamia
2. Thales
3. Cartography
4. Vasco da Gama
5. Portugal
6. Ptolemy
7. Amerigo Vespucci
8. Exploration
9. Compass

The letters in the vertical rectangle spell "Marco Polo."

Chapter 2

1. latitude
2. longitude
3. hemisphere
4. equator
5. projection
6. legend
7. scale
8. compass rose

Chapter 3

1. j
2. f
3. a
4. h
5. g
6. c
7. e
8. i
9. d
10. b

Chapter 4

1. e
2. g
3. c
4. f
5. b
6. d
7. a

Chapter 5

Across
6. pesticide
8. conservation
9. immigrant
10. natural resources (spelled without word space)

Down
1. globalization
2. forestry
3. drought
4. barter
5. cyclone
7. demographer

Chapter 6

Answers will vary; here are possibilities.

New England: water; ski lifts; Boston; lobster

Mid Atlantic: harbors; skyscrapers; New York City; potatoes

Southeast: bird life; dams; Atlanta; peanuts

Midwest: rich soil; steel plants; Detroit; dairy products

Southwest: oil; pueblos; Dallas; sugar beets

West: gold; Silicon Valley; Palo Alto; salmon

Hawaii: flowers; royal palace; Honolulu; pineapples

Alaska: gas; pipeline; Anchorage; salmon

Chapter 7

1. F
2. T
3. F
4. F
5. T
6. F
7. F
8. F
9. T
10. T

INDEX